Critical Guides to French Texts

Critical Guides to French Texts

EDITED BY ROGER LITTLE, WOLFGANG VAN EMDEN, DAVID WILLIAMS

LA ROCHEFOUCAULD

Maximes

D.J. Culpin

Lecturer in French,
University of St Andrews

Grant & Cutler Ltd
1995

© Grant & Cutler Ltd 1995

ISBN 0 7293 0385 3

1000700728 T

DEPÓSITO LEGAL: V. 4.792 - 1995

Printed in Spain by
Artes Gráficas Soler, S.A., Valencia
for
GRANT & CUTLER LTD
55-57 GREAT MARLBOROUGH STREET, LONDON WIV 2AY

Contents

Abbreviations

L	Letter
M	Maxime
ME	Maximes écartées
MS	Maximes supprimées
RD	Réflexions diverses

A Note on Editions of the 'Maximes'

Throughout the following chapters reference is made to the *Maximes et Réflexions diverses* edited by Jean Lafond in the Folio series and published by Gallimard. For the most part any edition of the *Maximes* may be used without difficulty, provided it follows the text and numbering of the fifth edition published by La Rochefoucauld in 1678. This is the case with all the principal editions currently available.

Modern editorial practice does differ, however, with regard to a number of additional maxims now usually included, in separate sections, after the 504 that constituted the edition of 1678. This supplementary material consists of some maxims which, after initial publication, La Rochefoucauld removed from subsequent editions (the *Maximes supprimées*), and others which he himself never published. The maxims of the second group are traditionally referred to as *Maximes posthumes*, but Lafond's edition is unique in that he renames them *Maximes écartées*. The rationale behind his designation is discussed in Chapter One. Lafond, like most other editors, also includes La Rochefoucauld's *Réflexions diverses*, which were not published during the author's lifetime.

More specialized editions of the maxims can be consulted by the reader who is looking for a fuller critical apparatus. In this respect Jacques Truchet's edition of the *Maximes* in the Classiques Garnier series is extremely valuable. It reproduces several early versions of the text, including the Liancourt manuscript, the pirated Dutch edition of 1664 and the first edition of 1665. Truchet also includes a number of letters written by La Rochefoucauld, Madame de Sablé and others which relate to the composition of the maxims. I have referred to these using the abbreviation 'L' followed by the number attached to each in the Classiques Garnier edition. Finally, the volume of *Œuvres complètes*, published in the Pléiade series, provides a fuller selection of La Rochefoucauld's letters and a more comprehensive chronological biography than either Lafond or Truchet. Full publication details of these and other useful editions are given in the bibliography, to which reference is made by italicized numbers in the text.

Introduction

The *Maximes* were not La Rochefoucauld's only excursion into the field of literature, but it is on this slender volume, barely eighty pages of printed text, that his literary reputation rests. That reputation is a curious one: the *Maximes* stand alongside Madame de Lafayette's *Princesse de Clèves* and Racine's tragedies as one of the landmarks of Classical French literature, enjoying a status consecrated by the inclusion of La Rochefoucauld among only a handful of writers to find a place in the prestigious Grands Ecrivains de la France series, published in the late nineteenth century.

But, since the appearance of the first edition in late 1664 or 1665, the *Maximes* have been more an object of contention than of uncritical admiration. Corrado Rosso sees the history of the reception of the *Maximes* in terms of a protracted judicial prosecution, and lists Diderot, Voltaire and Rousseau in the eighteenth century, Victor Cousin and Hippolyte Taine in the nineteenth, and Sartre and Camus in the twentieth among the major writers and intellectuals who have, in varying degrees, disparaged La Rochefoucauld's text (see *37*). Today, among students of French and for the French reading public, the *Maximes* are probably more known about than known, more read about than read.

The ambiguity of the critical response is largely the product of two factors. The first is the apparent pessimism of La Rochefoucauld's stance as a *moraliste*, or observer of human nature. The *Maximes* open with an epigraph in which he dismisses our virtues as, in most cases, 'des vices déguisés'; they end with an acknowledgement of the prominent place which has been given to 'la fausseté de tant de vertus apparentes' (M 504). In short, our moral shortcomings are largely unredeemed by compensating qualities. There is little to love or admire in men and women as depicted by La Rochefoucauld. He is, in the words of Diderot, 'le calomniateur de la nature humaine' (*37*, p.22).

The second cause for reticence is the maxim itself as a literary genre. The *Maximes* consist of 504 separate, often gnomic observations about human behaviour and motivation. The meaning and context of each remark receives only minimal elaboration, leaving to the reader the tasks of elucidation and synthesis. The maxim is, therefore, a difficult genre, and some readers have not been sure that the gains to be had from a close reading of the text are adequate compensation for the effort involved. Few critics would deny La Rochefoucauld's talent for polished and succinct expression. According to Gourdault, writing the biographical note for the Grands Ecrivains edition, La Rochefoucauld is to be appreciated for the quality of his 'mise en œuvre' rather than the originality of his ideas. But this is an acclamation of limited value, tantamount to the accusation, formulated by Camus, of empty word-play in which *forme* is given precedence over *fond*.

During the last half century, however, the critical response has become more nuanced. Scholars such as Truchet, van Delft and Lafond have attempted to elucidate the meaning of the *Maximes* by comparing the various published and unpublished versions of the text, and by situating the maxims within the ethical and theological context of the social milieu with which La Rochefoucauld was in contact. In doing so, they have highlighted greater subtlety and variety in the *Maximes* than has often been acknowledged by La Rochefoucauld's detractors.

The following chapters address a number of those topics around which critical debate has centred. They deal, respectively, with the context and development of the *Maximes*, La Rochefoucauld's view of the relationship between virtue and human nature, some of the major interpretations that have been offered of the text, and La Rochefoucauld's use of the maxim as a literary form. Together they constitute a survey of current critical thinking about the *Maximes*; but it is a survey coloured by my own view that the *Maximes* are, fundamentally, a satirical, even humorous text, and not the work of a bilious misanthropist.

1. Text and Context

When, in about 1659, La Rochefoucauld began work on what was to become the text of the *Maximes*, he was already forty-six years old. By that date he was living quietly in Paris at the Hôtel de Liancourt, the home of his uncle, the Duc de La Roche-Guyon. The tranquillity of this existence was in sharp contrast with the agitated life he had known during the previous three decades when he had been at the heart of the political intrigues and military conflicts by which France had been convulsed. Six years earlier, in 1653, he had begun work on his memoirs (published 1662), though these may be regarded not so much as a piece of creative writing as an attempt to justify his actions as a political rebel. The *Maximes* were, therefore, a new departure for La Rochefoucauld and their creation invites a number of questions. What sparked his interest in moral enquiry? Upon what sources did he draw for inspiration? Why did he choose the maxim as his preferred form of expression? How do we account for the note of disillusion that informs his observations?

François VI de La Rochefoucauld was born in 1613 into a noble family that traced its origins back to the eleventh century. Half a century before his birth La Rochefoucauld's forebears had fought prominently for both the Catholic and Protestant causes in the Wars of Religion. Until the death of his father in 1650 he was known as the Prince de Marcillac; subsequently he bore the title of Duc de La Rochefoucauld. His family history played a decisive role in shaping his attitudes and the course of his life. It was his desire to preserve the privileges of family and nobility that first provoked La Rochefoucauld's opposition to the policy of increasing royal power then being pursued by Richelieu, and in turn determined those allegiances which ultimately brought about his exclusion from the King's favour.

The narrative of his life until the early 1650s has all the

complexities and improbabilities of a baroque novel. In 1629, at the age of sixteen, La Rochefoucauld began a military career, fought campaigns in Italy and Flanders and was wounded at the battle of Mardick in 1646. At the same time he identified himself with the opposition to Richelieu and, in 1637, joined forces with the Duchesse de Chevreuse in an abortive plot to rescue the Queen from the influence of Richelieu by abducting her to Brussels. At the outbreak of the civil war known as the Frondes, which was provoked by Richelieu's attempt to establish royal absolutism, La Rochefoucauld joined the rebels under the Prince de Condé and was twice wounded, in 1649 and 1652, on the second occasion almost losing his sight. He also carried on a tempestuous and public affair with Madame de Longueville, Condé's sister, by whom he had a son, the Comte de Saint-Paul, in 1649.

La Rochefoucauld's fidelity to an aristocratic ideal of political independence brought him nothing but financial ruin and the failure of his social ambitions. The years following the cessation of hostilities were spent recovering his health, writing his *Mémoires* and restoring his family fortunes. In 1659 La Rochefoucauld wrote in his self-portrait: 'je suis mélancolique, et je le suis à un point que depuis trois ou quatre ans à peine m'a-t-on vu rire trois ou quatre fois' (5, p.222). That disposition had perhaps been reinforced by the experiences of the preceding years. The *Maximes* are, therefore, frequently read as the distillation of his experiences, a commentary upon themes such as the pursuit of power and the nature of love whose bitterness arises from the failure of his own ambitions.

In 1656 La Rochefoucauld returned to Paris, though it was not until 1659 that he was restored to the King's favour. Gradually he inserted himself into the social and literary life of the capital and of those salons which, after the turbulent years of the Frondes, served as meeting places where men and women of education and breeding could mingle freely with philosophers, scientists and *gens de lettres*. The salons of the 1650s and 1660s differed from each other in tone and composition: for example, the circle around Mademoiselle de Scudéry, authoress of historical romances including *Le Grand Cyrus* (1649-53) and *Clélie* (1654-60), is associated with the affectation and excessive refinement of preciosity; Madame de La Sablière's salon, frequented by the poet La Fontaine, was open to the philosophical discussions which opposed Descartes to the Epicurean philosopher Gassendi.

La Rochefoucauld's correspondence reveals that during the period 1659-1663, when the first maxims were being composed, he was particularly close to Madame de Sablé. Throughout the 1650s she had maintained a salon in the fashionable Place Royale that was especially noted for its gastronomic delights. But in 1659 she moved to a new home, adjoining the convent at Port-Royal de Paris, the stronghold of Jansenist theology in France, whose teachings on the vexed question of divine grace had been condemned by Pope Innocent X in 1653. In spite of her religious leanings Madame de Sablé did not entirely withdraw from the outside world, and her new circle included not only Pascal and Nicole from Port-Royal, but also Domat the jurist and aristocratic figures such as Monsieur le Prince, Rohan and Conti. It was therefore not exclusively theological, but united theologians, aristocrats. *érudits* and writers.

In spite of their differences, however, the various salons did have certain features in common, for the former *frondeurs*, political rebels like La Rochefoucauld himself, turned from the flamboyant pursuit of individual prestige to a more conformist code of manners and decorum known as *honnêteté*. The art of war was replaced by the art of conversation in which intelligence and lucidity became the weapons for prosecuting a close psychological analysis centring on motivation, sensibility and, above all, the nature of love. Though slightly reticent in manner, La Rochefoucauld possessed the qualities that fitted him for this social environment. The Chevalier de Méré, considered by his contemporaries an arbiter of good taste, himself describes La Rochefoucauld in a famous letter of 1687 as 'un si parfaitement honnête homme'. For example, to give an impression of La Rochefoucauld's skill as a conversationalist Méré simply reminds his reader: 'vous savez comment il s'en acquitte' (L 49). Nor did La Rochefoucauld stand aloof from the minor literary genres then in vogue in the salons. Madame de Montpensier's guests wrote short pen-portraits of themselves and others, the members of Mademoiselle de Scudéry's circle wrote poetry. In his own self-portrait, published in a collection of similar works and dedicated to Madame de Montpensier in 1659, he wrote: 'J'écris bien en prose, je fais bien en vers' (*5*, p.223). La Rochefoucauld's verse has not survived, but the *Maximes*, in their themes and style, are stamped with the hallmark of the society of which their author was a principal ornament.

The maxim did not exist as a literary genre before about 1650 (*38*, p.191). Some historical antecedents can be found, including the aphoristic formulations of traditional proverbs and the *Adages* of Erasmus (1500). More immediately influential was the enthusiasm for *sentences*, or notable sayings encapsulated in a brief but telling linguistic formulation which had persisted in literate society since at least the sixteenth century. The careful use of *sentences* is advocated, for example, by Corneille in his *Discours de l'utilité et des parties du poème dramatique* (1660). It can be seen in *Le Cid* where, in the specific context of her love for Rodrigue, the Infanta enunciates a general principle: 'Le seul mérite a droit de produire des flammes' (line 94).

The maxim as practised by La Rochefoucauld may also be considered as a development of other forms of salon literature. The members of Madame de Sablé's circle addressed themselves to the task of answering *questions d'amour*, such as these which were posed by the Marquis de Sourdis: 'S'il vaut mieux perdre une personne que l'on aime par la mort. que par l'infidélité?'; 'Si l'on peut aimer quelque chose plus que soi-même?'; 'Si l'amour peut être longtemps seul?'[1] Like the *Maximes*, they are enigmatic riddles which require for their formulation talents of psychological insight and verbal dexterity.

The maxims which constituted the first edition of La Rochefoucauld's text came into existence during a period of several years, beginning about 1659. The first official edition of the *Maximes*, dated 1665, opens with a long reflexion on the ubiquity of

---

[1] These questions are taken from a manuscript in the Bibliothèque Nationale, Fr. 17056, fol. 196. They are quoted in Guilleragues, *Lettres portugaises*, ed. Frédéric Deloffre (Paris, Gallimard, 1990), pp.31-32.

amour-propre (now MS 1) which had already been published by La Rochefoucauld, anonymously, early in 1660. Between 1659 and 1663 his letters bear witness to the systematic creation of *sentences* as part of the social life in the circles which he frequented. The new literary fashion became contagious, and he writes humorously to Madame de Sablé that 'l'envie de faire des sentences se gagne comme le rhume' (L 3). La Rochefoucauld's surviving correspondence includes versions of more than thirty maxims that ultimately found their way into the published text, some in a primitive form, others having already taken on their final shape.

In the early stages of composition La Rochefoucauld may have envisaged the creation of a composite work, to which he refers in a letter to his friend Jacques Esprit as 'notre volume' (L 4). The partners in this enterprise were Jacques Esprit himself, whose treatise entitled *La Fausseté des vertus humaines* (1677-78) develops themes similar to those of the *Maximes*, and Madame de Sablé, eighty-one of whose maxims were published posthumously in 1678. At that stage certain maxims seem to have been elaborated jointly by members of the group. The original authorship of some of them cannot, therefore, be established with accuracy. This is the case, for example, with maxim 260 of the first edition (MS 49) which opens with the phrase: 'La vérité est le fondement et la raison de la perfection, et de la beauté'. It is closely based on a maxim written by Esprit and preserved in one of La Rochefoucauld's own letters: 'La vérité est le fondement et la raison de la beauté' (L 2).

La Rochefoucauld himself became addicted to the composition of maxims, complaining in jocular tone to Esprit that he is 'à la merci des sentences' (L 6). While the enthusiasm of his collaborators waned, La Rochefoucauld discovered a growing facility for this form of expression and went on to independent literary creation. In consequence, as Henry Grubbs has shown, it is not possible to accept what was for many years the traditional view of La Rochefoucauld as a docile pupil responding to an impetus provided by Jacques Esprit and Madame de Sablé (*15*, p.482). In 1663 he jotted down what we know as maxim 36 in a post-script to Madame de Sablé, saying it came to him just as he was sealing his letter. He also notes his failure to maintain the detachment which was the hallmark of 'le vrai honnête homme' (M 203), observing ironically in himself the emergence of the pride which every author feels for his work (L 2 and L 20). By that time, what started out as a collaborative venture had become the product of a single creative mind.

The literary sources which may have fed La Rochefoucauld's moral vision are as difficult to identify with precision as the origins of the maxim as a literary form. Although La Rochefoucauld was an important player on the political and military stage, very little is known about his educational background or the environment which shaped his thinking. According to Segrais: 'Monsieur de La Rochefoucauld n'avait pas étudié', though this does not mean La Rochefoucauld was uneducated (*45*, t. I, p.17). In his self-portrait he refers to his enjoyment of reading: 'J'aime la lecture en général; celle où il se trouve quelque chose qui peut façonner l'esprit et fortifier l'âme est celle que j'aime le plus' (*5*, p.223). We have only limited information about the books La Rochefoucauld read or had in his possession, though it is possible to formulate a number of guarded hypotheses. The inventory of La Rochefoucauld's possessions at his Paris home, made after his death in 1680, includes 327 books, though the titles of only twenty-eight volumes are recorded (see *8*). However, since all of these books may subsequently have been taken to his château at Verteuil, it is perhaps possible to deduce the titles of the remainder from a similar catalogue drawn up there in 1728 following the death of François VIII de La Rochefoucauld (see *13*).

The range of titles appearing in the inventory of 1680 suggests that, at the very least, Segrais's comment about the limited range of La Rochefoucauld's educational background is misleading. There is no Bible mentioned, which is unusual for the time even in the case of someone who made no claims to devotion; but the list does include an Italian history of the Council of Trent in French translation, works on natural history and mathematics, travellers' tales, ancient history represented by Polybius and Tacitus in translation, the philosophical works of La Mothe Le Vayer, and the

1664 edition of Corneille's plays. The titles from the Verteuil catalogue which could have belonged to La Rochefoucauld include works by Horace, Plautus, Terence and Ovid, seventeenth-century novelists including d'Urfé and Madeleine de Scudéry, the plays of Molière and Racine, the poetry of Malherbe and La Fontaine as well as works of Spanish and Italian literature. These only confirm the picture that emerges from the inventory of 1680, a picture which shows La Rochefoucauld as a man whose literary culture was both eclectic and extensive.

The *Maximes* themselves contain no references to any writer or work with the exception of an unspecific mention of Seneca (MS 21) and an allusion to some verses in *Il Pastor fido* by the Italian poet Guarini (MS 33), both of which were removed after the first edition. Accusations of plagiarism were, however, not slow in coming. After perusing an early manuscript of the maxims prior to publication, one reader wrote to Madame de Sablé: 'cet écrit [...] n'est qu'une collection de plusieurs livres d'où l'on a choisi les sentences, les pointes et les choses qui avaient plus de rapport au dessein de celui qui a prétendu en faire un ouvrage considérable' (L 34). Another reader claims to identify a single source: 'La plupart de ces *Maximes* ont été prises d'un livre anglais assez mal traduit en français, intitulé: *La Sonde de la conscience* fait par un ministre anglais' (*4*, p.xxxviii, n.3). The work in question is *The Mystery of self-deceiving, or a discourse on the Deceitfulness of Man's heart*, by Daniel Dyke, published in 1615 and translated by Jean Verneuil in 1634. A similar claim was made by Ernest Jovy in 1910 (see *16*), though in fact there is little to substantiate it. La Rochefoucauld shares with Dyke a commonplace view of the catastrophic effects of *amour-propre* on human nature, but the English moralist has nothing to say about the influence of *fortune*, or circumstance, which so adds to the complexity of the *Maximes* (see *14*).

One other writer sometimes suggested as a major source of the *Maximes* is Baltasar Gracián whose *Oráculo manual*, subtitled *The Art of Prudence*, was published in 1647. The work was translated by Amelot de la Houssaie under the title *L'Homme de cour* in 1683;

but it was known in Spanish to Madame de Sablé before that date
and may, through her, have come to the attention of La Rochefoucauld. Gracián writes with the same disabused tone as La
Rochefoucauld. His 'art of prudence' depends on self-knowledge
and distrust of others. Self-interest is identified as every individual's
driving passion. There are in the *Maximes* several reminiscences of
La Rochefoucauld's Spanish predecessor (see *7*). Among them is
ME 49 which reads: 'Le sage trouve mieux son compte à ne point
s'engager qu'à vaincre'. It renders very closely a remark by Gracián
who had written that the man who takes reason as his guide 'estima
por más valor el no empeñarse que el vencer' (No.47). This was
translated by Amelot as: 'Celui qui a la raison pour guide [...]
trouve plus d'avantage à ne se point engager qu'à vaincre'. These
parallels, though intriguing, are not, however, sufficiently extensive
for the *Oráculo manual* to be considered a major source of the
Maximes.

The editors of the Grands Ecrivains edition identify a large
number of supposed sources for individual maxims, as does
E. Dreyfus-Brissac in *La Clef des Maximes de La Rochefoucauld*
(see *12*). Though some of the suggested *rapprochements* are valid,
others are simply chance linguistic similarities. Overall, the debt
which La Rochefoucauld owes to other writers is probably limited to
the generalized influence of those moralists whose works informed
the intellectual climate of the 1660s. Montaigne's *Essais* (for
example M 135 and MS 23) and Charron's treatise *De la sagesse*
(for example M 226) are among the more notable examples. The
Maximes can also be seen as a refutation of a treatise published by
La Mothe Le Vayer entitled *De la vertu des païens* (1642) which
supports the case for the authenticity of virtue outside a Christian
context. Lafond has argued that La Rochefoucauld's stance on this
issue, like that of his friend Jacques Esprit (formulated in *La
Fausseté des vertus humaines*) was profoundly marked by the
teaching of St Augustine. This contention will be examined in a
later chapter dealing with the interpretation of the *Maximes*.

In 1663 Madame de Sablé made copies of La Rochefoucauld's
maximes as they then existed and sent these out for a number of

people to read and comment upon. Four of these copies survive, and all list the same maxims in the same order. There are about 210 maxims included in each copy, though the maxims are not numbered and the paragraph divisions differ from one manuscript to another. Madame de Sablé's intention was, apparently, to test reaction to the maxims with a view to possible publication. A dozen letters survive, four from unknown respondents, which are more-or-less direct responses to Madame de Sablé's opinion poll. All bar one of these are preserved as copies made by Vallant, Madame de Sablé's secretary.

The opinions of Madame de Sablé's respondents were divided, though most were shocked by La Rochefoucauld's pessimistic view of human nature. The unfavourable response is exemplified by a letter from Madame de Maure, a friend of Madame de Sablé, in which she protests that the author 'fait à l'homme une âme trop laide' (L 27). Madame de Guyméné (another friend of Madame de Sablé and, like Madame de Maure, a devout Jansenist) even suggests that the corruption the author sees in others is simply a reflection of his own inner self. On the other hand, one anonymous respondent explains that, although one's first reaction might be unfavourable, a careful reading of the maxims leads to the opinion that 'il n'y a rien de plus fort, de plus véritable, de plus philosophe, ni même de plus chrétien' (L 31).

Madame de Sablé did her best at this point to prevent the manuscript from reaching a wider public, asking her correspondents not to copy the document and to reply as quickly as possible. This plan, however, seems to have gone awry. A pirated edition, possibly based on one of the copies she had circulated, was published shortly afterwards by Elzevier in Holland. It bears the date 1664 but may have been printed late in 1663 since La Rochefoucauld speaks of it in a letter to Thomas Esprit of 6 February 1664 as already having appeared. The volume bore the title *Sentences et Maximes de morale* but carried no author's name. It contained 188 maxims which were arranged by the editor according to theme but were not numbered.

The Dutch edition is referred to in the 'Avis au lecteur'

preceding the first official edition of the *Maximes*. This document
purports to have been written by the publisher but is almost
certainly from La Rochefoucauld's pen. In it the author complains
that he would not have made his work public had it not been
necessary to correct 'une méchante copie qui en a couru, et qui a
passé même depuis quelque temps en Hollande' (5, p.260). For
many years no such Dutch edition could be found and La
Rochefoucauld's remark was attributed to the traditional false
modesty of an author whose real intention is to side-step any
unfavourable criticism provoked by his work. But he was vindicated
in 1879 by the Belgian scholar Willems who discovered and
published a study of what has proved an extremely rare edition.

The first edition of the *Maximes* published by La
Rochefoucauld bears the date 1665, although it actually appeared
towards the end of 1664. It contained 317 maxims, of which the
last, which remains the concluding remark in the definitive edition,
was not numbered. The maxims are not grouped thematically as
they had been in the Dutch edition, but follow each other in an
apparently random manner. La Rochefoucauld insists in the 'Avis
au lecteur' that he has deliberately refrained from such grouping,
'de crainte d'ennuyer le lecteur'. Instead he refers his reader to an
alphabetical subject index which lists topics such as 'Sur l'amour',
'Sur l'honnête homme' and 'Sur la modération'.

The table of contents in the first edition was neither complete
nor entirely accurate. It was modified in subsequent editions and has
been expanded into larger indexes by modern editors. These show
the range of topics covered by La Rochefoucauld and the existence
of small clusters of maxims on an identical theme. For example,
taking the numbering of the definitive edition, we find 5 to 12 on
the passions, 114 to 129 on treachery and betrayal, and 137 to 142
on life in society. Also clearly visible is the preponderance of a
relatively small number of topics, largely related to the subjects of
virtue and human nature, including *amitié, amour-propre, défauts,
esprit, femmes, fortune, intérêt, mérite, paraître, passions* and
vertus.

La Rochefoucauld took the opportunity offered by the first

edition to answer the criticisms of his maxims that had already been voiced by the participants in Madame de Sablé's *sondage*. Mindful of those who see in his pessimism an heretical refutation of that Christian charity which makes possible acts of truly disinterested virtue, La Rochefoucauld cites authoritative precedents. The message of the *Maximes*, he claims in the 'Avis au lecteur', 'n'est autre chose que l'abrégé d'une morale conforme aux pensées de plusieurs Pères de l'Eglise' (5, p.260). The same points are made in a prefatory *Discours* written by Henri de La Chapelle-Bessé, a young lawyer, using arguments which La Rochefoucauld himself supplied via Thomas Esprit (L 39). But the *Discours*, which is encumbered with notes and written in the pedantic style of an academic treatise, clearly displeased La Rochefoucauld and was not subsequently republished (see L 40). From the second edition onwards the *Maximes* are introduced only by a modified 'Avis au lecteur' which says simply that 'on ne pourrait leur faire plus de tort que de se persuader qu'elles eussent besoin d'apologie' (5, p.41).

The lengthy evolution of the maxims themselves did not end with the 1665 edition. Four further editions followed during La Rochefoucauld's lifetime, in 1666, 1671, 1674 (dated 1675) and 1678. In the process the text underwent considerable modification, giving the lie to the notion that La Rochefoucauld was, as La Chapelle-Bessé had suggested in his *Discours*, only an amateur and not an author 'qui écrit de profession, qui s'en fait une affaire, et qui songe à s'en faire honneur' (5, p.262). The most obvious change is the increase in the number of maxims: this actually fell from 317 in the first edition to 302 in the second, but then grew to 341, 413 and finally 504. In each case the new maxims are added at the end of the previous edition. At the same time a process of selection and elimination was also taking place. Seventy-four maxims were suppressed after having been published in one or other of the editions, the most drastic pruning taking place after the first edition, from which sixty were removed. In some cases the reasons for their removal may be guessed at: MS 1 was perhaps too long, MS 58 lacked clarity, while MS 40 and MS 68 may have been politically insensitive, offering an implied criticism of Louis XIV. Other modifications which La Rochefoucauld introduced in subsequent editions will be examined in later chapters; these modifications include the exclusion of most references to religious notions such as God and immortality (Chapter Three), and the limitations which he introduced to the universality of his condemnatory moral judgements (Chapter Four).

This continuous process of modification finally produced, over a period of twenty years, the 504 maxims contained in the fifth edition of 1678. This was the last edition to be published in La Rochefoucauld's lifetime. It is regarded as the definitive edition and is usually the version reprinted today. Though the text itself has remained unchanged since that date, it is often now accompanied by variant readings taken from both the pirated Dutch edition and from manuscripts of the *Maximes* which have subsequently come to light. The manuscripts in particular give an indication of the development of the maxims before publication in much the same way as the first five editions illustrate their post-publication evolution.

Three of the most important manuscripts were first edited in the second half of the nineteenth century. In 1863 Edouard de Barthélemy published an edition of the *Maximes* based on a manuscript provided by the family of La Rochefoucauld and which, he claimed, was written in La Rochefoucauld's own hand. Three years later Gilbert published a version of the text in the Grands Ecrivains de la France series, based on another manuscript also supplied by La Rochefoucauld's family and which was again, apparently, autograph. Then, in 1883, the general editor of the Grands Ecrivains series decided to revise the volumes devoted to La Rochefoucauld. He found that both the manuscripts on which Gilbert and Barthélemy had based their work had disappeared. In their place he was supplied, again by the family of La Rochefoucauld, with a third manuscript, known as the Liancourt manuscript, which was also partially autograph. A photographic facsimile of this document was published by J. Marchand in 1931, but the manuscript itself was subsequently stolen. Since that time none of the three versions just mentioned has reappeared. It is impossible to say with certainty to what stage in the development of the *Maximes* these and other surviving manuscripts belong. Some, such as the copy contained in the Smith-Lesouëf collection at the Bibliothèque Nationale, may derive from the copies made by Madame de Sablé in 1663. Jacques Truchet has postulated that the Liancourt manuscript was possibly a primitive copy on which La Rochefoucauld recorded the maxims as they were written, between about 1659 and 1664 (see *4*, pp.383-401).

Modern editions of the *Maximes* also usually include a number of maxims in addition to the 504 of the fifth edition. These are divided into two groups which, since the Grands Ecrivains edition, have been known as *Maximes supprimées* and *Maximes posthumes*. Whilst the text of the 1678 edition is definitive, differences do occur in the numbering and the text of these additional maxims depending on the criteria operated by the individual editor. Truchet, Lafond and Martin-Chauffier (who follows the Grands Ecrivains edition) all differ in this respect, though concordance tables allow easy cross-reference between editions.

There is less disagreement about the *Maximes supprimées*, which were first published as a separate category in 1789. Unlike the maxims of the second group, the *Maximes supprimées* were actually published by La Rochefoucauld and then removed by him from subsequent editions. Editors have therefore differed principally only in deciding whether a maxim was really suppressed after publication or rather re-worked and published later in a modified form. The maxims traditionally known as *Maximes posthumes*, however, raise problems of a different order. A small number are taken from letters written by him to Madame de Sablé and Madame de Rohan (L 43 and L 44). Most of the remainder come in almost equal numbers from two principal sources: manuscript versions of the *Maximes* such as the *manuscrit de Liancourt* (which gives twenty-four maxims not found in any published version) and a supplement to the sixth edition of the maxims published after La Rochefoucauld's death, in 1693. This supplement contained fifty maxims, of which only half were, in fact, previously unpublished.

The maxims in the second additional category were labelled

Maximes posthumes by Gilbert in the belief that they had been written between the fifth edition of 1678 and La Rochefoucauld's death in 1680, and that they had been intended for publication. In fact he was mistaken on both counts. Truchet has shown that they date, in all probability, from 1671-74 when La Rochefoucauld was preparing the fourth edition, but from which they were ultimately excluded. Furthermore, several of the maxims taken from the *manuscrit de Liancourt* are not strictly posthumous in that they had previously appeared in the Dutch edition of 1664 (e.g. ME 1-3). Lafond's presentation of the text makes clear that these maxims date from the whole of the period during which La Rochefoucauld was writing maxims; but, unlike the *Maximes supprimées*, the *Maximes écartées* are those which he chose not to publish. The authenticity of every maxim included under this heading cannot be guaranteed with equal conviction, particularly ME 26 and ME 27 which are attested by no source other than the unauthorized Dutch edition. With this restriction, however, the two final sections, together with the definitive edition of 1678, bring to about 635 the number of surviving maxims that can be attributed to La Rochefoucauld.

Most editions of the *Maximes* also include La Rochefoucauld's so-called *Réflexions diverses*. These consist of nineteen short essays with titles like 'Du vrai', 'De la societé' and 'De la conversation', followed by an appendix comprising portraits of Madame de Montespan, the Cardinal de Retz, the Comte d'Harcourt and remarks about the early life of Richelieu. The *Réflexions diverses* were never published by La Rochefoucauld himself and little is known about their composition. Seven of them appeared in 1731, the remainder being published by Barthélemy, Gilbert and Régnier towards the end of the nineteenth century.

The *Réflexions* differ from the maxims not just in length but also in tone, developing a more positive view of the values of *honnêteté* and the constraints of society. They offer a clear and well-crafted presentation of what are essentially commonplace precepts, little different from the advice on manners and etiquette given by Guez de Balzac or the Chevalier de Méré; but they lack the incision, irony and suggestive complexity which are the hallmarks of the *Maximes*. Nonetheless, they are not without interest for the reader of the maxims. Part of M 430 recurs in textually identical form in RD IX, as do others in recognizably similar terms, for example the well-known M 203 in RD XIII. At times, the *Réflexions diverses* offer a gloss on the meaning of the maxims. There are also interesting stylistic comparisons to be made for, as Jacques Truchet has pointed out, the maxim and the reflection were not, for La Rochefoucauld, entirely unrelated as literary forms: maxim 504, the last and the longest of the *Maximes*, was maintained through five editions of the text, but it might equally have been presented as a reflection entitled 'Du mépris de la mort'.

This, then, is the story of how La Rochefoucauld came to produce the 504 maxims contained in the definitive edition of 1678. Together they constitute a collection of essentially separate observations which were elaborated and compiled over a period of twenty years. They are, however, held together by a thematic unity that is most clearly visible in La Rochefoucauld's treatment of virtue and human nature.

2. Virtue and Human Nature

On 9 March 1665 there appeared in the *Journal des Savants* a short review of the recently published *Maximes*, written by Madame de Sablé. In it she identifies La Rochefoucauld's great skill as being to 'démêler la variété des sentiments du cœur de l'homme', presenting him as a gifted observer of humanity who reveals to his readers a myriad useful details of which they might otherwise have remained forever unaware (*4*, p.xxiv; cf. L 41). But, for the significance of La Rochefoucauld's observations on human nature to be fully apparent, they must be seen within the context of a contemporary debate which centred on the efficacy of the will and the nature of the passions.

Moral philosophy in the first half of the seventeenth century was dominated by the teaching of Stoicism which stressed the supremacy of the mind over the flesh. According to Stoic doctrine, knowledge of the good and the true comes to us through intuitive reason and, by the exercise of will power, we may successfully perform those actions which we know to be right. It is also possible, by the exercise of our will, to control or even subdue the sufferings of our body or the temptation to gratify those desires to which we are incited by the passions. As Descartes put it in the *Traité des passions* (1649), a man need never lack the 'volonté pour entreprendre et exécuter toutes les choses qu'il jugera être les meilleures' (Art. 153).

By the 1660s Stoicism was being increasingly called into question, and La Rochefoucauld aligns himself squarely with its critics. Its deficiency arises from what La Rochefoucauld sees as the relative impotence of reason, combined with our inability to follow its promptings. In the 'Avis au lecteur' preceding the first edition, La Rochefoucauld says that the *Maximes* 'traitent l'*amour-propre* de corrupteur de la raison'. This is complemented by a maxim to which Madame de Sévigné objected because of the implied pessimism of its judgement on human nature, in which La Rochefoucauld states: 'Nous n'avons pas assez de force pour suivre toute notre raison' (M 42). His target is clearly Stoicism. Seneca (*c.* 4 B.C.-A.D. 65), one of its major exponents, is cited in MS 21 as being among those philosophers whose false precepts serve only to build the edifice of human pride. Furthermore, the first four editions of the *Maximes* carried a frontispiece showing a bust of Seneca and a cherub who has stripped from the philosopher's face a mask of impassivity to reveal the suffering etched on his features, a suffering which no effort of will can control. The engraving carries the legend 'L'amour de la vérité' and emphasizes the message of the *Maximes*: we can neither contain nor control the passions of the heart.

By calling into question the validity of Stoicism La Rochefoucauld offers a critique of precisely those values to which he and his social class had subscribed in the years prior to the ignominious outcome of the Frondes. This critique, which Paul Bénichou has called 'la démolition du héros' (see *18*), seeks in particular to dethrone notions of *gloire* and chivalrous love. *Les grands hommes*, princes like Louis XIV and military leaders such as Condé and Turenne whom La Rochefoucauld mentions in M 198, should, theoretically, possess the necessary strength of will to subordinate self-interest to the pursuit of disinterested virtue. Those who live up to this ideal are said to act with *générosité*, and are inspired to noble actions which enhance that indispensable sense of personal or family honour known as *gloire*. But, according to La Rochefoucauld, what passes for heroic action is misnamed or sullied with ulterior motives. In a maxim which may be taken as a reference to the political manœuvrings of Louis XIV, and which La Rochefoucauld removed after the fourth edition, the moralist notes that 'prendre des provinces injustement s'appelle faire des conquêtes' (MS 68). Fine-sounding words are often just a screen for self-interest: *la clémence* (enjoined upon rulers by Seneca in *De clementia*) is merely a ploy to win political support (M 15), *générosité* is nothing but disguised ambition (M 246), while the spirit of reconciliation derives from a dubious mixture of motives including *crainte* and *lassitude* (M 82).

Those members of society who wield authority and power should embody a concept of heroic virtue which disinterestedly seeks the good of the other; but this is far from being the case: great men allow themselves to indulge great faults (M 190) and, apart from an extra dose of vanity, 'les héros sont faits comme les autres hommes' (M 24). The great have more power and influence than other members of society, and can wreak more misfortune on their fellows. But, in La Rochefoucauld's estimation, they can be given no immunity for their misdeeds, nor can they shelter behind a notion of *raison d'état* whereby the end is held to justify the means. He is quite categorical: 'La gloire des grands hommes se doit toujours mesurer aux moyens dont ils se sont servis pour l'acquérir' (M 157).

Nevertheless, though tarnished by the shortcomings of fallible men, there is nothing wrong with 'l'amour de la gloire' *per se*. It is one of the causes of that valour which is universally admired (M 213) and brave men, inspired by *gloire*, are able to face courageously the prospect of death which, if it can never be truly scorned (as La Rochefoucauld maintains), can at least be faced with fortitude (M 504). Bravery is, like *gloire*, much less disinterested than often appears to be the case; but it can be defined: 'La parfaite valeur est de faire sans témoins ce qu'on serait capable de faire devant tout le monde' (M 216). It remains as an ideal which never ceases to fire the imagination.

La Rochefoucauld is equally satirical and equally ambivalent in his attitude towards the notion of chivalrous love, which depends no less than heroic virtue upon the ability to master the passions. Woman is presented as an unattainable and pure goddess, the lover who seeks to win her binds himself by vows of eternal fidelity, and their feelings for each other are characterized by gentleness and the absence of self-interest. This notion, inherited from the medieval tradition of courtly love, was preserved into the seventeenth century in novels such as d'Urfe's *L'Astrée* (1607-27) which was much admired by La Rochefoucauld. But its presuppositions were increasingly mocked in the years when La Rochefoucauld was writing his *Maximes*. Boileau's *Dialogue des héros de roman*, written about 1666, pokes fun at the heroes of Madeleine de Scudéry's novels, while Racine in the preface to *Andromaque* (1667) defends the violence of Pyrrhus's feelings in that play by saying, satirically, that 'Pyrrhus n'avait pas lu nos romans'. The charge which these writers brought, supported by La Rochefoucauld, is that any understanding of love which rests on notions of chastity, fidelity and self-denial is simply unreal and takes no account of human nature.

Women, as depicted by La Rochefoucauld, are far from being the unattainable goddesses of medieval romance. He is quite lapidary in his formulations: 'Il y a peu d'honnêtes femmes qui ne soient lasses de leur métier' (M 367). There should be no mistake: *honnête femme* is here not the female equivalent of *honnête homme*; female *honnêteté* implies not breeding and distinction but chastity. Women are weak-willed and readily susceptible to temptation; those who are *honnêtes* are like hidden treasure, safe only because no one is looking for them (M 368). Even in these cases *honnêteté* stems not from moral principle but is flaunted coquettishly as an attribute that only adds to women's desirability. Some women, it is true, never indulge in a *galanterie*, but women that do rarely stop at one (M 73). Coquetry itself is instinctive for women: it is simply an occupation and does not necessarily imply any emotional involvement (M 277). So fundamental to female psychology is it that, according to a maxim introduced into the third edition, women can actually suppress their *passion* more easily than their *coquetterie*. This unflattering judgement is, however, modified in the fourth edition, where La Rochefoucauld remarks that envy is destroyed by true friendship and coquetry by true love (M 376).

Clearly, where women are coquettes love is not undying. Constancy cannot be promised or taken for granted. Examples of fidelity might be cited, but for these there are several possible explanations. The first takes the form of a paradox: 'La constance en amour est une inconstance perpétuelle' (M 175); that is, we find in the object of our affections a succession of different qualities to which we attach our attention in turn. This is a conveniently pragmatic solution in which morality turns to good account the perversities of human nature. The second explanation proposes that constancy is artificially achieved because 'l'on se fait un honneur d'être constant' (M 176). It springs from a sense of duty and, though it may produce the satisfactions of virtue performed, it brings little sensual delight.

Inconstancy implies volatility and change; love itself is a violent passion, a 'mouvement continuel' (M 75) very unlike the tranquillity of *tendresse* depicted by d'Urfé and Madeleine de Scudéry. To give oneself in love implies vulnerability, and the self, when wounded by rejection or deception, reacts violently. Love in the *Maximes*, as in *Andromaque*, more easily gives way to hate than to indifference. Hermione, spurned by Pyrrhus, is able to say: 'Ah! je l'ai trop aimé, pour ne le point haïr! (line 416). La Rochefoucauld asserts: 'Plus on aime une maîtresse, et plus on est près de la haïr' (M 111). The effects of love, La Rochefoucauld notes, resemble hatred more closely than friendship (M 72). The most redoutable of these effects is jealousy; it is born with love but often survives the demise of that emotion. La Rochefoucauld reputedly collaborated with Madame de Lafayette in writing *La Princesse de Clèves* (1678) and his remarks foreshadow the feelings experienced by the heroine of that novel who finds her greatest sufferings in the pangs caused by 'la jalousie avec toutes les horreurs dont elle peut être accompagnée' (*43*, p.65). According to the *Maximes*: 'La jalousie est le plus grand de tous les maux, et celui qui fait le moins de pitié aux personnes qui le causent' (M 503).

Yet, for all his strictures, La Rochefoucauld still finds something magical and unforgettable in the experience of love, particularly young love. Within the context of marriage, with its implications of familiarity and permanence, love loses its lustre: 'Il y a de bons mariages, mais il n'y en a point de délicieux' (M 113). Love belongs to people who are both *jeunes* and *belles*, even though youth is fevered and beauty is subject to decay (M 497, M 271). For all love's imperfections, the *grandes passions* provide moments of exaltation which are remembered with nostalgia. At the age of sixty-five La Rochefoucauld wrote in the fifth edition of the

Maximes: 'Ceux qui ont eu de grandes passions se trouvent toute leur vie heureux, et malheureux, d'en être guéris' (M 485).

La Rochefoucauld does not simply reveal the emptiness of the ideal to which his generation and his social class subscribed, he also isolates the cause. This he locates in the impotence of the will, whose controlling force is nullified by a number of factors, the most important of which is *amour-propre* or self-love. Other moralists of the seventeenth and eighteenth centuries, among them Pascal and Rousseau, were equally preoccupied with the notion of *amour-propre*. This derived much of its influence from St Augustine who, in his influential work *The City of God*, formulated the view that life is polarized around two opposing forms of love, love of God and love of self. La Rochefoucauld's view of the omnipresent and predatory nature of *amour-propre* is clearly stated in what was originally the opening maxim, now MS 1, which begins with an unambiguous definition: 'L'amour-propre est l'amour de soi-même et de toutes choses pour soi'. It is the antithesis of Christian charity, or unselfish love of one's neighbour, which alone can inspire the 'vertus chrétiennes' to which La Rochefoucauld refers in M 358. How such Christian virtues might be acquired is not, however, envisaged in the *Maximes*, and the term *charité* is removed from maxim 9, and elsewhere where it figured in earlier versions. The heroic virtues of the pre-Frondes years, of Corneille's tragedies and of d'Urfé's *L'Astrée*, may be noble ideals but they are, in reality, simply idealized fictions.

Moral choice and the efficacy of the will are affected not just by the subconscious operation of *amour-propre*, but by other constraining forces, notably circumstance and human nature: 'La fortune et l'humeur gouvernent le monde' (M 435). By *fortune* La Rochefoucauld does not mean wealth, which is designated by *les biens*, as in maxim 323; he is referring to good fortune or chance which brings about events and determines even the social station into which we are born. Fortune governs the consequences of our actions independent of our will, intention or expectation. It is unpredictable, even amoral in its operation, favouring some and hindering others without regard to justice or individual worth. It is similar to the notions of *hasard* (M 57) and *notre étoile* (M 165), the kindly or unfavourable star that guides our destiny.

Humeur is a biological concept inherited from antiquity, according to which the body contains four humours or fluids: phlegm, bile (which is yellow), blood and atrabile (or black bile). The predominance of any one of these in a person's make-up will render him, respectively, calm, quick to anger, optimistic or gloomy. The notion of the humours was still widespread in the seventeenth century and is found, for example, in Molière's *Le Misanthrope* (1666), subtitled *L'atrabilaire amoureux*. According to La Rochefoucauld, our *humeur* shapes the consequences of the events that are caused by *fortune* (M 47). It therefore plays a crucial role in the pattern of our lives. The only change that can be effected in *humeur* is brought about by age and the passage of time, to which it is subject (RD XVII, XVIII). Together *fortune* and *humeur* determine our character and the circumstances of our lives. Vice, virtue, wisdom, wealth and public acclaim depend not upon ourselves but on forces over which we have no control. We are their prisoners until they have run their course (M 297).

The inescapable presence of *amour-propre* in human relationships creates a world in which *apparences* and *paraître* dominate, rather than *vérité* and *sincérité*. La Rochefoucauld draws his own conclusion: 'Ainsi on peut dire que le monde n'est composé que de mines' (M 256). Society is a hostile place of confrontation which opposes the individual to others. The phrase 'les autres' translates the reality of La Rochefoucauld's moral vision. It occurs in the *Maximes* more than two dozen times in opposition to *soi-même* or *nous-mêmes*. La Rochefoucauld recalls the Hobbesian vision of man's primal state in which a war of each against all is pursued with ferocity beneath the veneer of social decorum. Friendship is merely 'un commerce' or trading relationship (M 83), love 'une passion de régner' (M 68) and society itself an artificial creation whose members are 'les dupes les uns des autres' (M 87). La Rochefoucauld is describing the world with all its flaws and imperfections, not offering a prescription for how things should be; but it appears, *de facto*, to be built on the Machiavellian model of an amoral pursuit of power, where an individual's greatest need is to avoid falling into the traps that other people set for him (M 117; see *17*).

There is, however, one individual who is able to turn to his own advantage the constraints of *amour-propre* and *fortune*. This is the *habile homme* whose intelligence has a degree of cunning, for where others members of society are blindly driven by *intérêt* he governs his impulses so that, by calculation, he achieves greater personal advantage (M 66). He practises deception, claiming to despise ruses or stratagems only to make the more effective use of them at some opportune moment (M 124). Most people are not successful if they try to deceive, to play a part, to be other than they really are (M 115): we cannot pretend to be in love if we are not, or *vice versa*; we can never entirely conceal the accent of the place where we were born (M 342). The case of the *habile homme* is therefore all the more remarkable since, as La Rochefoucauld points out, 'C'est une grande habileté que de savoir cacher son habileté' (M 205). Similarly it is possible, by the use of cunning or *industrie*, to make the most of one's circumstances and turn even unexpected twists of fate to advantage. This is, in fact, an indispensable talent for those who would be truly great: 'Pour être un grand homme, il faut savoir profiter de toute sa fortune' (M 343).

Although apparently so sceptical about the likelihood of achieving virtue in practice, La Rochefoucauld suggests in the *Réflexions diverses* that some people instinctively have good taste 'parce que leur amour-propre et leur humeur ne prévalent point sur leurs lumières naturelles' (RD X). Elsewhere he comments that those who wish to excel by their own talents 'jugeraient des choses par leurs lumières, et s'y attacheraient par raison' (RD XIII). *Lumières naturelles* and *raison* are one and the same thing. Unfortunately, even when we perceive that some course of action is morally desirable we are not certain to perform it. Reason itself lacks the vigour necessary for effective action (M 469). A further ingredient is required. Paradoxically that ingredient is passion which, for all its dangers, has the capacity to stir, elevate and enlighten.

The passions were regarded with suspicion by many philosophers, among them Descartes, as well as by traditional Christian moralists, who saw in the passions, if not a source of evil, at least a disruptive force whose insistent clamour all too easily drowns out the voice of reason or the voice of God. However, the increasing rejection of Stoicism led not only to the belief that passion cannot be controlled, but also that it should not be suppressed in every situation. Fontenelle, in his *Nouveaux Dialogues des morts* (1683) sees the passions as the indispensable driving force of action: 'Les passions sont chez les hommes des vents qui sont nécessaires, pour mettre tout en mouvement, quoiqu'ils causent souvent des orages' (*42*, p.261). La Rochefoucauld does not deny the threat to moral rectitude that is posed by the power of the passions: for him the passions are the only orators whose persuasion is always effective (M 8). If we are able to resist a particular passion it is only because that passion is weak, not because we are strong. But his attitude towards the passions is ambivalent.

La Rochefoucauld divides passions into two types, the *violentes passions* and those which might be called *languissantes* (M 266). The former are often considered by moralists and theologians to be the most pernicious, but La Rochefoucauld regards them with a degree of indulgence since, though tending to excess, they have a strength which arises from *grandeur d'âme*. He sums up this paradox in his self-portrait, published in 1659: 'J'approuve extrêmement les belles passions: elles marquent la grandeur de l'âme, et quoique dans les inquiétudes qu'elles donnent il y ait quelque chose de contraire à la sévère sagesse, elles s'accommodent si bien d'ailleurs avec la plus austère vertu que je crois qu'on ne les saurait condamner avec justice' (*5*, pp.225-26). Magnanimity too is the product of 'grandeur d'âme'. 'La magnanimité', says La Rochefoucauld, 'est assez définie par son nom' (M 285): that is *magna anima* or greatness of soul. Likewise, we are compelled to admire *l'amour de la gloire* and *la parfaite valeur*, which, though vitiated, are born of the same source. Greatness of soul is the hallmark of the truly *grand homme*.

It is in the more docile states of soul that La Rochefoucauld sees greater danger. He says, for example, of *la paresse*: 'elle usurpe sur tous les desseins et sur toutes les actions de la vie; elle y détruit et y consume insensiblement les passions et les vertus' (M 266). Idleness appears innocuous, but eats away both virtue and passion itself. It is the antithesis of *activité* and *ardeur* (M 293). *Bonté* in general, and *modération* in particular stem, according to La Rochefoucauld, from simple inertia rather than from a positive commitment to reason and virtue. They derive, like cowardice, avarice and weakness, from lack of vision and an absence of moral fortitude. Though La Rochefoucauld undermines the integrity of many virtues, weakness is the only vice which he considers irremediable: 'La faiblesse est le seul défaut que l'on ne saurait corriger' (M 130). Consequently, his greatest disdain is reserved, not for *les grands* who commit great moral indiscretions, but for 'les fous et les sottes gens' (M 414) who lack the individuality to assert themselves for either good or ill.

The *violentes passions*, such as love and ambition, are those which nullify the efficacy of the will and are traditionally most associated with disorder. But La Rochefoucauld's endorsement of *force* and his condemnation of *faiblesse* imply a corollary which he does not shrink from making: no one should be praised for virtue unless he possesses the force to be evil, but which he restrains (M 237). Energy itself may excite a certain admiration, irrespective of the morality of the end to which it is directed: 'Il y a des héros en mal comme en bien' (M 185). According to the *Maximes*, we each possess latent talents and insights that are liberated only by the spontaneity of passion:

> Il semble que la nature ait caché dans le fond de notre esprit des talents et une habileté que nous ne connaissons pas; les passions seules ont le droit de les mettre au jour, et de nous donner quelquefois des vues plus certaines et plus achevées que l'art ne saurait faire. (M 404)

There is a curious wisdom in giving oneself up to the fever of passion. In this context La Rochefoucauld attaches a sense to the terms *fou* and *folie* which is not entirely pejorative. Recalling Erasmus's treatise *In Praise of Folly* (1511), he writes: 'Qui vit sans folie n'est pas si sage qu'il croit' (M 209; see *27*).

La Rochefoucauld spends most of his time unmasking what, in the final maxim, he calls our 'vertus apparentes'; but he allows us to glimpse the theoretical existence of certain positive values that are not tarnished by self-interest (see *26*). If, for example, there is such a thing as a truly pure love it is 'celui qui est caché au fond du cœur, et que nous ignorons nous-mêmes' (M 69). By implication it is aroused not by the calculating operation of the intellect, but by the spontaneity that is proper to the heart. Similarly there are other qualities which are not normally visible: they are either unusual or their existence is to be inferred from the counterfeit versions of them with which we are familiar. True love is rare, true friendship even rarer; but that is not to say they do not exist (M 473). Likewise 'la véritable bonté' (M 481). There is also at least some possibility of being born 'sans envie' (M 433), whilst hypocrisy implies the reality of those virtues which it attempts to imitate (M 218).

Such virtues are, however, only glimpsed as a theoretical possibility. In their absence we must be content with those values which Jean Starobinski has called 'morales substitutives' (see *32*). What passes for virtue generally arises from impure motives (M 200). But, because the maintenance of society is dependent upon the operation of standards based either on virtue or the semblance of virtue, motivation is less important than the actions to which it gives rise. It is therefore possible to affirm: 'Il y a des faussetés déguisées qui représentent si bien la vérité que ce serait mal juger que de ne s'y pas laisser tromper' (M 282). There are times when it is appropriate to accept counterfeit coinage in place of the real thing.

La Rochefoucauld concedes the possibility of disinterested virtue, but only in those rare cases where an individual is obedient to the voice of reason, transformed by divinely inspired *charité*, or driven by the spontaneity of passion. With these exceptions he rejects the authenticity of the moral code based on *dépassement de soi* to which his own social élite had subscribed, pointing to flaws which undermine the integrity of *gloire* and heroic love. In its place he substitutes a value system based on a combination of pragmatism and *grandeur d'âme* which, because they do not depend on absolute standards of behaviour, carry with them implications of amorality. In effect he thereby reinstates the values of his class since moral grandeur is reserved for those of birth and breeding; it is the antithesis of that restraint which is synonymous both with conservative bourgeois morality and traditional Christian virtue.

In short, La Rochefoucauld's moral code possesses a complexity that, from earliest times to the present, has fostered the diverse and contradictory interpretations to which the *Maximes* have given rise.

3. Intentions and Interpretations

The *Maximes* are not a moral or philosophical treatise. They develop no closely constructed argument and state no clear conclusion. Even when compared with other works emanating from Port-Royal and its Jansenist sympathizers the difference is palpable. Pascal in his *Pensées* leads the sceptic progressively to the point where, having recognized the wretchedness of his godless state, he is ready to take a leap of faith; Jacques Esprit's *La Fausseté des vertus humaines* boldly states its thesis on the title page. La Rochefoucauld's approach is more oblique, and the epigraph, which appeared for the first time in the fourth edition, provides the reader with only the most tenuous orientation: 'Nos vertus ne sont, le plus souvent, que des vices déguisés'. The frontispiece and a handful of maxims indicate the writer's distaste for a particular philosophy which is powerless in the face of suffering and death (M 22 and M 504), namely Stoicism. But the moral, philosophical or religious standpoint from which La Rochefoucauld launches his criticism of disinterested virtue, and his intention in doing so, remain obscure.

The *Maximes* have always aroused diverse responses and differing interpretations, many of which were anticipated in the replies to Madame de Sablé's *consultation* of 1663. In the account of the *Maximes* which Madame de Sablé published in the *Journal des Savants* she wrote that it had already provoked 'des jugements bien différents' (*4*, p.xxiv). An original version of her review, included in a letter to La Rochefoucauld of 18 February 1665, elaborates on these divergent opinions in two paragraphs which were subsequently removed. On the one hand, she explains, 'Les uns croient que c'est outrager les hommes que d'en faire une si terrible peinture'; conversely, 'Les autres au contraire trouvent ce traité fort utile' (L 42).

The arguments advanced by those who censured La

Rochefoucauld are not without justification. It is perfectly possible to read the maxims as the expression of religious scepticism, linking their author with the *libertins* or *esprits forts* whose views were gaining greater currency among the *honnêtes gens* during the second half of the century. This is the implication of the view taken by Madame de Schonberg whom La Rochefoucauld had known for many years and, as Mademoiselle de Hautefort, had planned to abduct with the Queen in 1637. She writes to Mme de Sablé: 'après la lecture de cet écrit, l'on demeure persuadé qu'il n'y a ni vice ni vertu à rien, et que l'on fait nécessairement toutes les actions de la vie' (L 30). The nub of her criticism is the notion of moral necessity, implicit in the *Maximes*, which robs mankind of all freedom of action. The original versions of what later became maxims 153 and 297 locate the impulse to all action in *fortune* and *humeur*, fate and temperament. In short, as La Rochefoucauld put it in the opening words of maxim 43: 'L'homme croit souvent se conduire lorsqu'il est conduit'. But if there is no possibility of moral choice or resistance to evil there can likewise be no concept of moral responsibility. Such a view has religious implications, for where man is not to be blamed for his sins he has no need of redemption or forgiveness.

The importance attached by La Rochefoucauld to the notions of *fortune* and *humeur* may be seen as implying a philosophical determinism which sets man at the level of the rest of creation, governed by physical laws in a universe which has no place for God. This impression is reinforced by the almost total absence of a religious dimension to La Rochefoucauld's moral analysis. The copies made by Madame de Sablé in 1663 and the Dutch edition of 1664 contained a number of maxims referring to God, providence and charity, but these are either excluded from La Rochefoucauld's own published version of the text or are modified in such a way as to remove the theological element. For example, the Dutch edition contains a maxim which reads, 'Il n'y a que Dieu qui sache si un procédé est net, sincère et honnête'. In its definitive form (M 178 in the first edition, M 170 thereafter) this becomes: 'Il est difficile de juger si un procédé net, sincère et honnête est un effet de probité ou d'habileté'.[2] Only a small number of maxims remain which make overt reference to religion or invoke specifically theological concepts such as 'la malignité de notre nature' (M 230), 'le salut' (M 241), 'les vertus chrétiennes' (M 358) and 'la dévotion' (M 427).

In particular, La Rochefoucauld makes no mention of divine providence, that is God's intervention in the chain of cause and effect, guiding creation for the working out of his own purposes. The only such reference is found in MS 39 which states that all events are part of the divine plan, but this maxim was removed after the first edition and is not found in any of the extant manuscripts. One can, therefore, understand the hostility of an unnamed respondent who wrote to Madame de Sablé: 'on peut dire qu'entre les mains de personnes libertines ou qui auraient de la pente aux opinions nouvelles, que cet écrit les pourrait confirmer dans leur erreur, et leur faire croire qu'il n'y a point du tout de vertu' (L 34). From this the same writer concludes that the *Maximes* are positively dangerous.

However, the case for the moral utility and orthodoxy of the *Maximes* can also be put with some force. Other moralists, including Pascal and Esprit, have made similar observations about the servitudes by which man's will is limited, but without being subject to the criticism of immorality levelled against La Rochefoucauld. For Pascal, human nature and custom are the forces which, whether we like it or not, effectively shape our decision-making processes. He even fears that human nature might itself be only 'une première coutume, comme la coutume est une seconde nature' (*44*, No.126). For Jacques Esprit too, man is subject to compulsion, unable to stop 'le cours des humeurs qui règnent en lui, et qui font naître en lui successivement tant d'affections et de dispositions différentes' (*41*, t.I, pp.70-71). The reason Pascal and Esprit escape censure is that their observations are intended to apply

---

[2] *Maximes* 9, 37, 65 and 170 have been modified to remove any religious reference, as have *Maximes supprimées* 25 and 33. The *Maximes écartées* 8, 10, 20, 34 and 37 retain their specifically religious tone but were never published by La Rochefoucauld.

only to unregenerate men and women, to those who are not released from their enslavement to custom and personality by the intervention of divine grace. The Christian reader will accept that the moralist's pessimism is well-founded, knowing that it is only part of the total picture.

The *Maximes* too can be situated within this theological context as Jean Lafond, prominent among modern scholars, has persuasively argued (see *28*). Several of those readers who responded positively to the *Maximes* in Madame de Sablé's *consultation* originally interpreted them in this way. One unknown writer says the work exposes the futility of human wisdom, revealing the power of original sin and the malignity of human nature 'quand il s'agit de soi-même sans l'esprit de Dieu' (L 31). Madame de Liancourt is also ready to acknowledge that there are good things in the maxims, 'pourvu qu'on ôte l'équivoque qui fait confondre les vraies vertus avec les fausses' (L 33). On this reading La Rochefoucauld's only fault is that he does not make his meaning sufficiently clear. Another of Madame de Sablé's respondents is therefore correct when she claims that 'le chrétien commence où votre philosophe finit' (L 35).

From the first edition of the *Maximes* onwards, La Rochefoucauld himself encouraged this interpretation of his work. In the 'Avis au lecteur' he states that their message is 'conforme aux pensées de plusieurs Pères de l'Eglise' (*5*, p.260). This should be understood as referring particularly to St Augustine whose writings played a dominant role in seventeenth-century theology, influencing Christian groups of all persuasions and notably the Jansenists at Port-Royal. Many of Augustine's writings owed their origin to the Pelagian heresy of the early fifth century which stressed the efficacy of free-will, claiming for it a role even in the initiation of religious conversion. Augustine's writings are, therefore, directly concerned with the issues of original sin and divine grace. As understood by Cornelius Jansen and re-formulated by him in his *Augustinus* (posth. 1640), they formed the substance of Jansenist belief and the chief weapon of the Jansenists in their battle against the perceived semi-Pelagianism of the Jesuits. The

Jansenists held the view that, as a result of original sin, the actions
of all unregenerate men are governed by love of self, *amour-propre*.
In consequence, God's commands cannot be fulfilled by mankind
unless He bestows special grace on each individual. In those to
whom grace is denied any appearance of virtue is purely illusory;
they are the prisoners of their passions and subject to what may be
called natural determinism.

In 1664, following the publication of the Dutch edition, La
Rochefoucauld wrote to le Père Thomas Esprit, brother of Jacques
Esprit, who was himself in contact with Madame de Liancourt and
the convent of Port-Royal. In his letter he explains that the maxims
are harmless since their purpose is to prove that the much vaunted
virtue of the ancient pagan philosophers had no substance, and
could not have done since it did not spring from Christian faith. He
goes on to underline the poverty and contradictions of the human
heart, concluding that mankind's greatest need, in all things, is to
be 'redressé par le christianisme' (L 39; cf. 5, p.270).

The prefatory *Discours*, published with the first edition,
develops the same line of argument. La Chapelle-Bessé states that
La Rochefoucauld's pessimistic appraisal of human virtue is not
applicable to all men: 'c'est de l'homme abandonné à sa conduite
qu'il parle, et non pas du chrétien' (5, p.264). In subsequent
editions the reference to the Church Fathers, contained in the
'Avis', was replaced by a phrase giving a more specific orientation
to the reader's understanding. Speaking in the guise of the
'libraire', La Rochefoucauld says that the author of the *Maximes* has
considered mankind only 'dans cet état déplorable de la nature
corrumpue par le péché'. His analysis is, therefore, not applicable to
those in whom God is at work 'par une grâce particulière' (5, p.41).

The first edition of the *Maximes* opened with a denunciation
of self-love: it ended, as it still does, with a maxim in which La
Rochefoucauld denounces 'la fausseté de tant de vertus apparentes'.
His terminology and moral analysis may, therefore, be seen as a
reflection of an Augustinian or Jansenist view of unregenerate man
who, lacking the support of divine grace, cannot attain to acts of
real virtue. In that case, when La Rochefoucauld says that *souvent*

or *presque toujours* acts of apparent virtue are really flawed, he is allowing for the exceptional case of those true Christians whose lives have been transformed by divine power. The 'vertus apparentes' (M 504) contrast with the 'vertus chrétiennes' of maxim 358 which are made possible by that humility which is the product of grace.

However, the arguments in favour of an Augustinian interpretation of the text have not met with universal acceptance. A number of objections can be alleged. La Rochefoucauld's relationship with Madame de Sablé, Jacques Esprit and other supporters of Port-Royal is explicable without supposing him to have been in sympathy with their theological views. The Jansenists were regarded with suspicion by the King, who saw in their refusal to accept religious censure a threat to the absolutism of his own authority. It has even been suggested that the independent outlook of the Jansenists made them sympathetic to the political aspirations of the *frondeurs* with whom La Rochefoucauld was associated.[3] Furthermore, the letter to Thomas Esprit, the 'Discours' and the 'Avis au lecteur' do not have to be accepted uncritically as evidence in favour of the Augustinian interpretation. They constitute an attempt, by La Rochefoucauld, to guarantee his own orthodoxy and ensure a defence against the potentially dangerous charge of *libertinage*. We are no more obliged to believe La Rochefoucauld in these circumstances than we are to accept Molière's protestations of religious sincerity in the preface to *Le Tartuffe*. Finally, the Augustinian thesis is obliged to dismiss a large number of maxims as irrelevant to the author's central purpose. According to Jean Lafond: 'Bon nombre de réflexions sur les femmes, l'amour, le monde ou l'esprit, n'ont qu'un rapport assez lâche, ou n'ont aucun rapport, avec la ligne générale des *Maximes*' (5, pp.25-26). In short, Augustinianism opens up illuminating perspectives on the *Maximes*,

---

[3] See Richard M. Golden, *The Godly Rebellion: Parisian curés and the religious Fronde, 1652-1662* (Chapel Hill, NC: The University of North Carolina Press, 1981). Gérard Ferreyrolles (*Pascal et la raison du politique*, Paris, Presses Universitaires de France, 1984) disputes the extent to which Jansenists supported the Frondist position.

but is inadequate as a total explanation of their meaning.

Other critics place at the very centre of the *Maximes* La Rochefoucauld's preoccupation with the intellectual and emotional issues arising from an individual's insertion into the social milieu which Lafond refers to as 'le monde'. Paul Bénichou, for example, does not find in the *Maximes* a theologically inspired analysis of human nature but an 'art de vivre profane' (*19*, p.29). Similarly, Louis van Delft believes La Rochefoucauld is best described as a 'moraliste mondain' whose preoccupations are those of the *honnêtes gens* inhabiting the Paris salons (see *22* and *23*). His values are shaped by the needs and possibilities of individuals in society, not by the requirements of religion.

The author of the *Maximes* may not believe in more than the occasional manifestation of truly disinterested virtue, but he subscribes to a code of *honnêteté* that governs the external veneer of good manners in polite society. Human beings must find ways of living harmoniously together and of limiting the consequences of their mutually predatory *amour-propre*. For this purpose they adopt conventions of decorum whose modern origins go back to Castiglione's *Book of the Courtier* (1528) and which, in La Rochefoucauld's day, were elaborated by the Chevalier de Méré in short essays with titles such as *De la vraie honnêteté* and *De l'éloquence et de l'entretien* (posth. 1701). The constraints of *honnêteté* are acknowledged to be artificial, but they offer a *modus vivendi* which holds out the possibility of social cohesion. At best they may actually encourage a moral renewal based on authenticity and sincerity.

La Rochefoucauld understands that society is both a necessary and a fragile construction. In the second of the *Réflexions diverses*, entitled 'De la société', he sets out the nature of the problem: 'Il serait inutile de dire combien la société est nécessaire aux hommes: tous la désirent et tous la cherchent, mais peu se servent des moyens de la rendre agréable et de la faire durer'. Society is the place in which we can find pleasure or happiness. The problem is our inability to achieve the necessary self-denial: 'Chacun veut trouver son plaisir et ses avantages aux dépens des autres'.

An indication of how society may become possible is found in La Rochefoucauld's definition of the perfect *honnête homme*. According to maxim 203: 'Le vrai honnête homme est celui qui ne se pique de rien'. He is not a *savant* and will not lay claim to any specialist expertise, just as La Rochefoucauld himself attempts to dispel the picture of himself as an author who deliberately writes with a view to publication. Instead, he presents himself as a generalist. As Pascal puts it in the *Pensées*: 'Cette qualité universelle me plaît seul' (*44*, No.647). That is why, in an essay entitled *Sur les sciences où peut s'appliquer un honnête homme* (1666), Saint-Evremond excludes mathematics and philosophy as suitable subjects of study. La Rochefoucauld excludes religion. The *honnête homme* is not a pedant, still less a theologian: he may hold to the articles of faith but avoid in his conversation such subjects as might sow contention and division. Hence the absence of this topic from the *Maximes*.

Honnêteté is an essentially pragmatic doctrine. It was widely understood as a social ethic which governed external questions of appearance and decorum but did not necessarily imply standards of moral rectitude. This was recognized by Pascal who was a friend of Méré and who (in spite of his admiration for the universality of the *honnête homme*) wrote scathingly of rules of social etiquette which leave man's fundamental moral nature unreformed. According to the *Pensées*: 'On a fondé et tiré de la concupiscence des règles admirables de police, de morale et de justice. Mais dans le fond, ce vilain fond de l'homme, ce *figmentum malum* n'est que couvert. Il n'est pas ôté' (*44*, No.211).

La Rochefoucauld adopts a more accommodating stance. Instead of an ethical system built on moral absolutes he accepts the reality of self-interest and constructs a theory of social relations which is the product of what Bénichou calls 'amour-propre policé' and which acknowledges the utility of evil (*19*, p.33). In reality most apparent virtues are, as we saw in the last chapter, 'des faussetés déguisées', but, for practical purposes, they have the value of absolute truths (M 282). Maxim 182 can be seen as an expression of this position: 'Les vices entrent dans la composition des vertus comme les poisons entrent dans la composition des remèdes. La prudence les assemble et les tempère, et elle s'en sert utilement contre les maux de la vie'. Prudence is the key to personal happiness and social stability. Yet, because prudence itself is dependent upon self-control, it is, as La Rochefoucauld knows, a fragile foundation on which to construct so great an edifice (M 65). But La Rochefoucauld acknowledges the realities of social existence and would have endorsed the advice given by Philinte, in Molière's *Le Misanthrope*, to the uncompromising and anti-social Alceste: 'Mon Dieu! des mœurs du temps mettons-nous moins en peine, / Et faisons un peu grâce à la nature humaine' (lines 145-46). It is not with the inadequacies of *honnêteté* that La Rochefoucauld finds fault so much as with the *malhonnête homme* or the *ingrat* who infringes the rules that this doctrine prescribes.

Paradoxically, however, the true *honnête homme*, as understood by La Rochefoucauld, is committed to a quest for authenticity, lucidity and sincerity. The elegance of speech and bearing dictated by *honnêteté* must, above all, be marked by 'le naturel'. But the harder we try to act naturally the less natural we become: 'Rien n'empêche tant d'être naturel que l'envie de le paraître' (M 431). La Rochefoucauld resolves the dilemma through self-knowledge: to avoid affectation and be natural we must first know our own character. He explains the situation in his *Réflexion* 'De l'air et des manières': 'Il y a un air qui convient à la figure et aux talents de chaque personne; on perd toujours quand on le quitte pour en prendre un autre. Il faut essayer de connaître celui qui nous est naturel, n'en point sortir, et le perfectionner autant qu'il nous est possible' (RD III). From self-knowledge it is a short step to sincerity: 'Les faux honnêtes gens sont ceux qui déguisent leurs défauts aux autres et à eux-mêmes. Les vrais honnêtes gens sont ceux qui les connaissent parfaitement et les confessent' (M 202). But, since in his analysis of man's moral nature La Rochefoucauld identified *faiblesse* as the source of those defects which he finds most repugnant, it is no surprise to learn that the weak-minded cannot be sincere (M 316). Sincerity requires a *grandeur d'âme* which is attainable only by those who are truly *honnêtes gens*.

La Rochefoucauld's *morale mondaine* offers the means of attaining whatever degree of happiness is ultimately compatible with the human condition. Society is a place of masks and deceptive appearances (M 256), in which it is possible to survive by consciously subscribing to the impostures of *honnêteté* as a practical *modus vivendi*. Yet, in underlining the value of sincerity, *honnêteté* also points towards an alternative vision of society in which individuals are no longer prey to the predatory *amour-propre* of others (see *20*). Pascal asserts as a commonplace of moral philosophy that: 'Tous les hommes recherchent d'être heureux'; they differ only in their conception of happiness (*44*, No.148). La Rochefoucauld is pragmatic in this regard: 'c'est par avoir ce qu'on aime qu'on est heureux, et non par avoir ce que les autres trouvent aimables' (M 48). Happiness, like politics, is the art of the possible, and it is La Rochefoucauld's realization that *bonheur* is inseparable from the compromises of social existence that makes him, as Bénichou has said, 'un des théoriciens de l'honnêteté' (*19*, p.36).

The three interpretations of the *Maximes* that we have examined, the sceptical, the Augustinian, the socially pragmatic, do not exhaust the different readings of the text which have been offered. Louis Hippeau, for example, has seen in La Rochefoucauld's moral code a reflection of Epicureanism, which constituted one variety of scepticism that was gaining acceptance in the second half of the seventeenth century (see *25*). Hippeau's analysis has not found universal critical acceptance, but this scholarly disagreement serves to highlight the diversity of inspiration underlying the *Maximes*, a diversity which makes possible almost as many interpretations of the text as there are readers. In the eighteenth century, for example, when atheism was widespread among the *philosophes*, the early judgement of the *Maximes* as both gloomy and dangerous was stood on its head. Helvétius, expounding in *De l'esprit* (1758) an ethical system based on utilitarianism and self-interest, refers to La Rochefoucauld's vision of *amour-propre* as the expression of a kindly personality. For over three hundred years diverse interpretations have been offered of La Rochefoucauld and his enigmatic *Maximes*. *Libertin, augustinien, mondain, épicurien*: which label fits best? The answer surely is, as Louis van Delft has suggested, that 'La Rochefoucauld n'appartient à aucune école' (*23*, p.146).

The inherent ambiguity of the text cannot, however, be dissociated from the nature of the maxim as a literary form. No interpretation of the *Maximes* can disregard the internal structure of La Rochefoucauld's individual remarks or the linguistic formulations which he commonly employs.

4. The Maxim

Apart from judgements about the ethical implication of the *Maximes*, many of the early readers commented upon the author's style, which they found striking and unusual, not to say unnatural. One unknown reader, whose comments were transmitted to Madame de Sablé, observes that the *Maximes* depend rather heavily for their effect upon the use of paradox (L 31). Another reader objects that, having borrowed the substance of his book from a host of other authors, La Rochefoucauld has also taken over their *pointes*, or literary conceits, of which his work is full. More recently, Albert Camus has written that La Rochefoucauld allowed his preoccupation with form to dictate and distort the accuracy of his content. From this he concludes that 'il est bien difficile d'apprendre quelque chose sur la conduite des hommes en lisant les maximes de La Rochefoucauld' (*40*, p.6). The style and structure of the *Maximes* have, in effect, been central to their reception by generations of readers.

In the 1660s the maxim had only just come into existence as a literary genre in its own right, and there remained a certain ambiguity both about its form and even about the terminology by which it should be described. In the letters written by Madame de Sablé, Jacques Esprit and La Rochefoucauld himself during the composition of the *Maximes*, their productions are referred to interchangeably as both 'sentences' and 'maximes', though the latter term occurs with greater frequency as the time of publication approaches. The first edition itself carries the title *Réflexions ou Maximes morales* which, in subsequent editions, becomes *Réflexions ou Sentences et Maximes morales*. La Chapelle-Bessé is aware of the confusion, referring to 'Les *Réflexions*, ou si vous voulez les *Maximes* et les *Sentences*, comme le monde a nommé celles-ci'.

Furetière's dictionary of 1694 reveals the prevailing hesitation over terminology. Under the heading 'Maxime' we read: 'Principe, fondement de quelque art ou science. C'est une *maxime* d'état ... Machiavel établit des maximes dangereuses dans sa politique'. That is to say, a maxim is simply a political, moral or artistic principle, and is not inherently associated with brevity of expression. Much nearer to what we now understand as a maxim is the term 'Sentence', which is defined by Furetière as a 'Dit notable, parole qui porte un grand sens, une belle moralité'. But the terminological ambiguity is underlined by the following phrase, added by way of amplification: 'Ces belles maximes qui sont dans les poètes et les historiens sont marquées comme *sentences* en gros caractères, afin qu'on les retienne mieux'. His definition of 'Réflexion' brings us full circle. In its figurative sense it means, he says, the 'méditations qu'on fait sur quelque chose', and, by way of amplification, he adds: 'Les *Réflexions* morales de Mr. de la Rochefoucauld'.

Philip Lewis points to one important difference between the *réflexion* and the *maxime*: the reflection puts its emphasis on content while the maxim draws attention to its form or the style in which it is written (see *35*). For most commentators brevity is central to what might be called the specificity of the maxim. Madame de Maure compliments Madame de Sablé's own maxims precisely because they have what she calls 'ce tour court que j'aime aux sentences' (L 28). When La Chapelle-Bessé answers the criticism that the meaning of some of La Rochefoucauld's maxims is obscure he makes the same point: maxims must be written 'dans un style serré' which implies both density and brevity (*5*, p.267).

The title that La Rochefoucauld gives to his collection of maxims, *Réflexions ou Sentences et Maximes morales*, is ambiguous, suggesting identity rather than difference between the three terms mentioned. But it has the virtue of embracing the stylistic diversity of the *Maximes*, which could not all be described as brief or compressed formulations. Thirty-nine maxims are five or more lines long, representing almost 8% of the total number. Of these, number 504 is two and a half pages long, 233 and 215 are each one page long and 139 is half a page in length. These 'maxims' are semantically and linguistically complex utterances, consisting of several sentences or clauses. Maxim 264, for example, begins with a statement about the self-interested nature of pity; this is followed by an explanation of the writer's meaning, an illustration of his precept, and an amplification of its consequences. All that is missing is the conclusion, which the reader must supply for himself.

Nevertheless the majority of the *Maximes* are characterized by the brevity commended by Madame de Maure. They are typically a single sentence comprising a statement or definition without explanation, illustration or amplification. One such maxim offers a definition of eloquence: 'La véritable éloquence consiste à dire tout ce qu'il faut, et à ne dire que ce qu'il faut' (M 250). Eloquence is inseparable from a fixed concentration on the essentials of discourse, a pruning of superfluity and redundance. A similar movement towards brevity and concentration can be seen in La Rochefoucauld's shaping of his text as it passed through successive editions. For example maxim 75, on the subject of prudence, is over one hundred and sixty words long in the first edition; as number 65 in the second to fourth editions it is reduced to just over forty words, shrinking again to just twenty-three words in the edition of 1678.

The effects of the changes introduced by La Rochefoucauld can be seen in the epigraph, which originally appeared in the first edition and read as follows:

Nous sommes préoccupés *de telle sorte* en notre faveur
que ce que nous prenons pour des vertus n'est *en effet*
qu'*un nombre de* vices qui leur ressemblent, et que
l'orgueil et l'amour-propre nous *ont déguisés.*
(CLXXXI)[4]

In the second edition changes were made to the words printed in italics, changes which together achieve greater brevity and immediacy. In the second and third editions the maxim is printed as

---

[4] Roman numerals refer to the first edition of the *Maximes* as given in Truchet's edition (see *4*).

number 172 in the following form:

> Nous sommes si préoccupés en notre faveur que souvent
> ce que nous prenons pour des vertus n'est que des vices
> qui leur ressemblent, et que l'amour-propre nous
> déguise.

In the fourth edition we find this maxim not only in the body of the
text in the form just quoted, but also standing as the epigraph, in a
further modified form. Here La Rochefoucauld has identified the
essential core of his observation, from which all accretions are
stripped:

> Nos vertus ne sont, le plus souvent, que des vices
> déguisés.

As the epigraph, the maxim remained unchanged in the fifth edition
but was removed from the body of the text.

Many of La Rochefoucauld's maxims are constructed according to a small number of formulae which have all the ubiquity of the
moralist's preoccupation with *amour-propre*. Particularly common
is the use of a binary structure which balances the two halves of a
single utterance. This may take the form of two contrasting nouns
which are placed for emphasis at the beginning and the end of the
maxim, as for example *humeur* and *fortune* in maxim 47: 'Notre
humeur met le prix à tout ce qui nous vient de la fortune'.
Particularly frequent is the elaboration of an antithesis, as between
esprit and *cœur* in maxim 102: 'L'esprit est toujours la dupe du
cœur'. Sometimes the two elements constitute a comparison, as
between the notions of *se défier* and *être trompé* created by the use
of *plus ... que* in maxim 84: 'Il est plus honteux de se défier de ses
amis que d'en être trompé'. Often the comparison or antithesis is
organized around a central conjunction such as *mais, et* or
néanmoins. Corrado Rosso has estimated that antithesis is used in
seventy per cent of all the maxims (*38*, p.188).

The shortest of the *Maximes* commonly take the form of a

categorical statement, a pronouncement by the author: for example M 42, 'Nous n'avons pas assez de force pour suivre toute notre raison'. The tone is authoritative, even authoritarian; but its very assertiveness invites commentary and contradiction. Who is meant by *nous*, and are there no exceptions? The verb is not qualified by an adverb or adverbial phrase, so do we always lack the strength to follow our reason, or just sometimes? In many cases the simplest statement is presented in the form of a definition. Some of these relate to specific attributes: 'La modération est ...' (M 18), 'La sincérité est ...' (M 62), 'La flatterie est ...' (M 158). Others are applied to particular groups of people: 'La clémence des princes n'est que ...' (M 15), 'La constance des sages n'est que ...' (M 20). In such cases the tense of the verb suggests not just the present of immediacy but also that of eternal truth. This heightens the impression that La Rochefoucauld is simply stating the rules governing human behaviour and that these rules allow no possibility of variation.

In subsequent editions a number of changes introduced by La Rochefoucauld had the effect of attenuating the universality of his judgements. In 1664 several maxims already contained a word or phrase suggesting that there are, however rarely, exceptions to his gloomy assessment of human nature. Maxim CXLI (139 in the fifth edition) claims that 'il n'y a quasi personne qui ne pense plutôt à ce qu'il veut dire qu'à répondre précisément à ce qu'on lui dit'. But the incidence of restrictive terms such as *quasi* increases with the passage of time. 'Il semble que' (M 36), 'en la plupart des hommes' (M 78), 'd'ordinaire' (M 146), 'peut-être' (M 7), 'presque' (M 10) and 'souvent' are all employed in this way. Of these the last is the most common, being added to more than a dozen maxims. For example, maxim 97 in the first edition, beginning 'L'homme est conduit, lorsqu'il croit se conduire', becomes number 43 in the second edition and reads: 'L'homme croit souvent se conduire lorsqu'il est conduit'. By introducing these restrictions La Rochefoucauld appears to be responding to the criticism, referred to by La Chapelle-Bessé, which had been made by those readers who objected that 'les Maximes sont presque partout trop générales'.

But, as the writer of the *Discours* put it, there is a limit to the degree of attenuation that can be introduced into the *Maximes* 'sans leur ôter tout le sel et toute la force' (*5*, p.268).

The *Maximes* appear both spare and abstract in execution, but in fact they contain a surprising degree of discreetly used rhetorical ornamentation, notably metaphor and simile. Metaphor is the application of descriptive terms to an object to which those terms are not literally applicable. For example maxim 228 ('L'orgueil ne veut pas devoir, et l'amour-propre ne veut pas payer') imagines pride owing and self-love paying in a way that is only metaphorically possible. Similarly, La Rochefoucauld speaks of jealousy feeding on doubt (M 32) and self-interest speaking many languages (M 39). In the majority of cases these metaphors are associated with *amour-propre*, pride and self-interest, those attributes of character most particularly denounced by the *Maximes*. *Amour-propre* in maxim 2 is described as a flatterer and in maxim 4 as an 'habile homme': it schemes to achieve its own ends (M 83) and can blind or enlighten its victims at will (M 494). Metaphor may take an extended form , as in maxim 3 which speaks of 'le pays de l'amour-propre' where there are still many 'terres inconnues'; or it may pass almost unnoticed, as in the case of 'l'esprit' which is always 'la dupe du cœur' (M 102). Overall there are several dozen metaphors in the *Maximes*. Their effect is almost to personify the sinister qualities they describe, giving them a graphic realization and a sense of omnipresence which emphasizes their ceaseless and irresistible activity.

Simile is like metaphor, except that here the relationship between objects or attributes is made clear by the presence of a word such as *comme*: 'L'absence diminue les médiocres passions, et augmente les grandes, comme le vent éteint les bougies et allume le feu' (M 276). As with metaphor, La Rochefoucauld's similes undermine surface appearances to reveal complexity and instability. Maxim 171, for example, returns to the geographical image already found in maxim 3: 'Les vertus se perdent dans l'intérêt, comme les fleuves se perdent dans la mer'. Where the two attributes juxtaposed by the simile are unexpected the result is a sudden touch of humour.

This is the case with the similarity La Rochefoucauld discovers between true love and ghostly apparitions: 'tout le monde en parle, mais peu de gens en ont vu' (M 76). Humour is noticeably present in the case of similes relating to people rather than abstract attributes such as constancy (M 21) or the 'maladies de l'âme' (M 193). Some individuals are described as being like popular songs that are sung for a short while and then, by implication, forgotten (M 211). The moralist even makes a rare reference to the concerns of ordinary life, comparing 'la reconnaissance' (respect that is paid to others) with 'la bonne foi des marchands': both are useful for purely pragmatic reasons, the former facilitating social relations, the latter encouraging trade (M 223). Other similes are drawn from architecture (M 292), warfare (M 504) and medicine (M 182). They reveal in La Rochefoucauld a taste for what Jacques Truchet calls 'l'image insolite' and spring from a humorous view of human failings (*4*, p.liv).

Humour is, in fact, integral to La Rochefoucauld's vision of social relations and to his practice of the maxim. As such it deserves wider consideration than it is commonly given. The editors of the major critical editions of the *Maximes* which are currently available differ considerably in their appreciation of the place of humour in La Rochefoucauld's work. L. Martin-Chauffier in the Pléiade edition elaborates the traditional picture of the cheerless pessimist whose disillusion has been fuelled by the collapse of his own ambition and whose outlook is indelibly marked by 'l'amertume et la misanthropie' (*2*, p.293). Jacques Truchet in the Garnier edition is less reductive in his reading of the text. He maintains that it would be wrong always to take La Rochefoucauld seriously, suggesting that, on the contrary, 'il s'amuse souvent, probablement plus souvent qu'il ne le laisse voir' (*4*, p.lvi). For his part Jean Lafond, writing in the preface to the Folio edition of the text, acknowledges that, within the *Maximes* themselves: 'L'angle d'attaque est sans doute fréquemment celui de la satire'; but he confines the use of humour to a number of reflexions on 'les femmes, l'amour, le monde ou l'esprit' which, as we saw in Chapter Three, are, in his view, only loosely connected to the central theme of the *Maximes* (5, pp.25-26).

La Rochefoucauld himself comments on the role and utility of humour in social life. According to the second of the *Réflexions diverses* ('De la societé'): 'Il y a une sorte de politesse qui est nécessaire dans le commerce des honnêtes gens; elle leur fait entendre raillerie'. The *honnêtes gens* do not take offence at *raillerie* which, in *Réflexion* XVI ('De la différence des esprits'), he also calls *la moquerie*. In the same *Réflexion* La Rochefoucauld says it is perfectly possible for a person to have 'un air sérieux' and still say things which are 'enjouées' or witty. He tells us in his self-portrait that he is by temperament 'mélancolique'; he likes serious conversation and yet, he adds, 'je sais la goûter aussi quand elle est enjouée'.

According to *Réflexion* II, 'la raillerie' has a particular attribute: '[elle] fait voir en ridicule les objets qui se présentent'. La Rochefoucauld observes an element of the ridiculous in everyone, even the most *honnête*: 'S'il y a des hommes dont le ridicule n'ait jamais paru, c'est qu'on ne l'a pas bien cherché' (M 311). As Molière famously put it in *La Critique de l'Ecole des femmes* (1663): 'il n'est pas incompatible qu'une personne soit ridicule en de certaines choses, et honnête homme en d'autres' (scene VI). Molière believed mockery to be a legitimate weapon in the artist's hands, and wrote, in the Preface to *Les Précieuses ridicules* (1659), of 'la satire honnête et permise' which he felt entitled to use in ridiculing folly. La Rochefoucauld is aware that mockery carries with it the danger of giving offence, but adds in similar vein: 'La moquerie peut néanmoins être permise, quand elle n'est mêlée d'aucune malignité'. He also knows that 'la raillerie' can be morose or humorous in tone, a difference which he attributes to the greater or lesser degree of 'âpreté' in the personality of the observer (RD XVI). Mockery is, therefore, a permissible but potentially dangerous ingredient in social relationships, and is described in the *Maximes écartées* as 'un poison qui tout pur éteint l'amitié et excite la haine' (ME 27). It is a useful corrective which may be considered one of 'les poisons [qui] entrent dans la composition des remèdes' (M 182).

The maxim is the perfect literary vehicle for humour, particularly in the form of wit, or *esprit*: not unnaturally for, as Shakespeare's Polonius observed, 'brevity is the soul of wit'. *Esprit* is an intellectual form of the comic, in which delight or amusement is derived from the unexpected association of thought and expression. It is a device to be handled with caution which, at its best, creates new insights, and, at its worst, degenerates into a brilliant but meaningless display of verbal pyrotechnics. Wit is an aristocratic rather than a popular form of humour, dependent both upon the verbal dexterity of the speaker who formulates his message and the intelligence of the listener who decodes its meaning. During the seventeenth century *esprit* flourished in the Paris salons, from the aristocratic *chambre bleue* of the Marquise de Rambouillet to the *ruelle* of Madeleine de Scudéry. The neologisms and striking expressions to which it gave rise are preserved in a wide range of literature, from Molière's satirical *Précieuses ridicules* to the more restrained pages of Madame de Lafayette's *Princesse de Clèves*. La Rochefoucauld's cultivation of brevity and his use, in the *Maximes*, of rhetorical devices such as metaphor and simile justify the remark made by Madame de Schonberg in 1663 that 'il y a en cet ouvrage beaucoup d'esprit' (L 30).

La Rochefoucauld's wit is barbed with irony. As a comic form irony is understated and, unlike farce and burlesque, relies on suggestion for its effect. It is a subtly humorous perception of inconsistency in which an apparently innocuous observation is undermined so as to give it a very different significance. Maxim 19 is of this type: 'Nous avons tous assez de force pour supporter les maux d'autrui'. The apparent confirmation that we do possess some *force* unexpectedly collapses: the degree of strength is belittled if it can support the ills of others and, by implication, not our own. Such force is also suspect in kind, since it finds satisfaction in the misfortunes of others, misfortunes which we observe with perverse pleasure, but which we cannot (or will not) remedy. The maxim therefore suggests paradox, which, as has already been noted, is as widespread in the *Maximes* as irony itself (see 21).

The irony in the maxims is most readily apparent where there is an obvious discrepancy between a traditional role or pattern of behaviour assigned to an individual and the unexpected reality suggested by the moralist. This is the case with many of the maxims describing lovers (M 312), old men (M 93) and coquettes, for example maxim 367 ('Il y a peu d'honnêtes femmes qui ne soient lasses de leur métier'), which reduces chastity from the level of binding moral absolute to that of tiresome social convention. But it is equally possible to see humour rather than bitterness in other maxims, such as those concerned with *amour-propre*, that are usually given a more pessimistic reading. 'L'amour-propre est le plus grand de tous les flatteurs' (M 2) can be read either as an expression of tolerant amusement or of disenchanted condemnation. In this case our aesthetic appreciation of the *Maximes* may depend on which of the ethical interpretations outlined in the last chapter we find most plausible. Jean Lafond sees in La Rochefoucauld's condemnation of *amour-propre* a reflection of the austerity of his Augustinian inspiration and minimizes the place of humour in the *Maximes*. Conversely, those critics who see La Rochefoucauld as a *moraliste mondain* find in his work a pragmatic social ethic which suggests, not condemnation, but a good-natured, if disabused, acceptance of human weakness.

The frontispiece may supply some orientation to our interpretation. This takes the form of a denunciation of the hypocritical wisdom of Stoic philosophers as represented by Seneca. The bust of the philosopher surmounts a base on which are inscribed the words 'Quid vetat'. These are abbreviated from a verse by Horace which reads 'ridentem dicere verum Quid vetat?', meaning: 'What prevents the laughing man from telling the truth?' The moralist need not have a long face: his goal of unmasking folly can be achieved by *raillerie*. To take this view fundamentally alters our reading of the *Maximes*; it also provides a further explanation for the exclusion by La Rochefoucauld of all maxims dealing with religion: as Molière discovered with *Le Tartuffe*, the institution least able to accommodate satire was the Church.

La Rochefoucauld's approach to questions of form and language makes it possible to situate him in relation to the broad trends of literary history and in particular to the notions of Baroque and Classicism which are widely used to describe succeeding periods of literary activity in seventeenth-century France. In *La Littérature de l'âge baroque*, which deals with the period 1580 to 1665, Jean Rousset points to the *Maximes* in illustration of the principal Baroque themes of disguise and inconstancy. The applicability of this critical label to La Rochefoucauld is, however, subject to caution. What Rousset calls 'le débat de l'être et du paraître' (*39*, p.226) is equally central to *La Princesse de Clèves*, but Madame de Lafayette's novel is not, for that reason, an example of the Baroque; nor does La Rochefoucauld's preoccupation with the ceaselessly changing forms of *amour-propre* necessarily make the *Maximes* a Baroque text. Theme and style must go together.

Stylistically the Baroque is characterized by flamboyance and exaggerated ornamentation. These are not characteristic of the later versions of La Rochefoucauld's text, but may be discerned in earlier or suppressed versions. Maxim 254 in the second and subsequent editions describes humility in metaphorical terms as a disguised form of pride 'qui s'abaisse pour s'élever'. In the first edition the same metaphor is more elaborately developed. Pride takes on all sorts of *figures*, but 'il faut avouer néanmoins qu'il n'est jamais si rare ni si extraordinaire que lorsqu'il se cache sous la forme et sous l'habit de l'humilité; car alors on le voit les yeux baissés, dans une contenance modeste et reposée: toutes ses paroles sont douces et respectueuses, pleines d'estime pour les autres et de dédain pour lui-même'. It is pride, La Rochefoucauld concludes, which plays all these parts (CCLXXVII). In a still earlier version of the same maxim, found in the Liancourt manuscript and the Dutch edition, there is a comparison between the many manifestations of pride and the sea god Proteus who could change his form at will. Lafond comments that 'Les métaphores sur le déguisement et l'évocation de Protée' give to these versions of maxim 254 a Baroque character that is also found in MS 1, the long maxim that was originally number one in the first edition.

In this case the comparison is exact. The structure of the suppressed maxim makes use of the rhetorical device of repetition which strives to produce its impact by a process of accumulation: 'L'amour-propre est l'amour de soi-même ... *il* rend les hommes idolâtres d'eux-mêmes ... *il* ne se repose jamais hors de soi ... *Rien* n'est si impétueux que ses désirs, *rien* de si caché que ses desseins, *rien* de si habile que ses conduites; *ses souplesses* ne se peuvent représenter, *ses transformations* passent celles des métamorphoses, et *ses raffinements* ceux de la chimie' (my italics). But the prolongation of the metaphor supplies only redundant details. There is no development of the central idea. Not so maxim 504 which, though of a similar length, develops and illustrates the central notion of 'la faussetée du mépris de la mort'. What we see in the *Maximes* is, therefore, a process of stylistic development on the part of La Rochefoucauld tending towards the brevity, restraint and rejection of exaggerated metaphor that were associated with French Classicism in the years between about 1660 and 1680 when the maxims were being written. In RD IV, 'De la conversation', La Rochefoucauld writes: 'Il y a de l'habileté à n'épuiser pas les sujets qu'on traite, et à laisser toujours aux autres quelque chose à penser et à dire'. Boileau, the supreme exponent of Classical orthodoxy, makes a similar observation in his *Art poétique* (1674), dismissing the sterile verbosity of an author who is unable to relinquish his subject 'sans l'épuiser' (I. 50). For this reason, perhaps, MS 1, with its Baroque characteristics, was suppressed after the first edition; maxim 504, though more of an extended *réflexion* than a maxim, retained its place at the conclusion of each edition.

La Rochefoucauld did not confine himself to writing within a single literary form: he practised extended prose in both the *Mémoires* and the *Réflexions diverses*; but it was in the compressed form of the maxim that he discovered both his true originality and the appropriate vehicle for his ironic vision of life. The *Maximes* are as complex aesthetically as they are thematically. Their form has been seen diversely as the product of an authoritarian age that seeks to impose a normative view of human behaviour, as a sort of salon game in which form is allowed to determine meaning, and as an appropriate literary format for conveying the discontinuities of existence (see *34* and *38*, pp.100-02). As a literary genre the maxim has much in common with poetry: in both, the words are heavily charged with a meaning or meanings whose elaboration is left to the reader. Above all, the *Maximes* are a work of literature, not of moral philosophy; and herein lies their value. As Lafond (quoting Proust) points out, 'plus important que la pensée, il y a "ce qui nous donne à penser" ' (*5*, p.27).

Conclusion

It is possible to read the *Maximes* as a document whose primary interest is historical, and which reflects the moral and aesthetic values of a society based on the Paris salons in the second half of the seventeenth century. La Rochefoucauld focuses on ethical questions of direct relevance to the social lives of the *honnêtes gens*, not on abstract issues of metaphysics. But for him, as for Racine and Madame de Lafayette, the moral optimism of the pre-Frondes years has evaporated, leaving in its place only an awareness of man's moral inadequacy. In aesthetic terms this vision is expressed with the brevity and restraint associated with Classicism and recommended by Boileau as the antidote to the prolixity of an earlier age.

Such a reading, though valid, is, however, also incomplete, for it ignores the literary value of the text and the relevance it may have for the modern reader. Jean Starobinski and W.G. Moore among modern critics assess the significance of the *Maximes* in broader terms, both of them referring to the 'complexité' of La Rochefoucauld (*33* and *29*, p.303). The author's analysis of virtue and of love, of the passions and *honnêteté* offers to the reader the surprise of the unexpected, blending a quixotic yearning for the ideal with a pragmatic acceptance of the possible. This complexity is the source of those divergent interpretations which, from earliest times to the present, have been offered of the *Maximes*. Augustinian, Epicurean, *libertin, mondain*, pessimistic and satirical are critical labels which highlight in turn some of the many facets of La Rochefoucauld's text.

The complexity of La Rochefoucauld's meaning is mediated by, and in part arises from, the specificity of the maxim. *Fond* cannot be dissociated from *forme*. The characteristic brevity of the *Maximes* and the acontextuality even of La Rochefoucauld's longer observations divorces them from any of the various intellectual and moral frameworks that might have supplied a definitive interpretation. Even apparently categorical *sentences* lack a sense of absolute closure: their confident though tendentious affirmations have frequently antagonized La Rochefoucauld's readers, but the emphasis which he places on *raillerie* as a necessary and permissible ingredient in social relations suggests that amusement rather than anger may have been his response to the inevitability of human weakness.

The maxim is a difficult form which will perhaps never capture more than a limited readership. But La Rochefoucauld's ability to combine richness in observation with artistry in execution gives to the *Maximes* an interest that surely transcends the particular historical moment in which they were written.

Select Bibliography

A comprehensive list of scholarly books and articles dedicated to the *Maximes* would be very extensive. With few exceptions, only items referred to in the preceding chapters are included here. Fuller critical bibliographies can be found in several of the books listed below, notably those by Jean Lafond (*28*), Philip Lewis (*35*) and Corrado Rosso (*37, 38*).

EDITIONS OF THE 'MAXIMES' AND OTHER WORKS BY LA ROCHEFOUCAULD

1. *Œuvres de La Rochefoucauld*, éd. D.L. Gilbert, J. Gourdault, A. et H. Régnier, 4 vols, album et appendix (Coll. des Grands Ecrivains de la France: Paris, Hachette, 1868-1893).
2. *Œuvres complètes*, édition établie par L. Martin-Chauffier, revue et augmentée par Jean Marchand (Bibl. de la Pléiade: Paris, Gallimard, 1964 [1957]).
3. *Réflexions ou sentences et maximes morales. Réflexions diverses*, 'Textes Littéraires Français', éd. Dominique Secrétan (Geneva, Droz, and Paris, Minard, 1967).
4. *Maximes*, texte établi, avec introduction, chronologie, bibliographie, notices, notes, documents sur la genèse du texte, tableau de concordance, glossaire et index par Jacques Truchet, 2e édition revue et corrigée (Classiques Garnier: Paris, Garnier, 1972 [1967]).
5. *Maximes et Réflexions diverses*, édition présentée, établie et annotée par Jean Lafond (Coll. Folio: Paris, Gallimard, 1976).
6. *Maximes*, éd. J. Truchet (Coll. GF: Paris, Garnier-Flammarion, 1977).

BIOGRAPHY AND CONTEXT

7. Baldensperger, Fernand, 'L'Arrière-plan espagnol des *Maximes* de La Rochefoucauld', *Revue de Littérature Comparée*, 16 (1936), 45-62.
8. Balmas, Enea, 'La Bibliothèque du duc de La Rochefoucauld', in *De Jean Lemaire de Belges à Jean Giraudoux. Mélanges offerts à Pierre Jourda* (Paris, Nizet, 1970), 179-201.
9. Bishop, Morris, *The Life and Adventures of La Rochefoucauld* (Ithaca, New York, Cornell University Press, 1951).

10. Coster, Adolphe, 'Baltasar Gracián, 1601-1658', *Revue Hispanique*, 29 (1913), 346-753.

11. Delft, Louis van, 'Madame de Sablé et Gracián', *Saggi e ricerche di letteratura*, 22 (1983), 265-85.

12. Dreyfus-Brissac, Edmond, *La Clef des Maximes de La Rochefoucauld* (Paris, chez l'auteur, 1904).

13. Gérard, Mireille, 'Le catalogue de la bibliothèque de La Rochefoucauld à Verteuil', in *Images de La Rochefoucauld. Actes du Tricentenaire 1680-1980*, ed. J. Lafond & J. Mesnard (Paris, Presses Universitaires de France, 1984), 239-92.

14. Grubbs, Henry A., 'The Originality of La Rochefoucauld's *Maximes*', *Revue d'Histoire Littéraire de la France*, 36 (1929), 18-59.

15. ———, 'La Genèse des *Maximes*', *Revue d'Histoire Littéraire de la France*, 39 (1932), 481-99; 40 (1933), 17-37.

16. Jovy, Ernest, *Deux inspirateurs peu connus des 'Maximes' de La Rochefoucauld, Daniel Dyke et Jean Verneuil* (Vitry-le-François, Tavernier, 1910).

INTERPRETATIONS

17. Baker, S.R., 'The Works of La Rochefoucauld in relation to Machiavellian ideas of morals and politics', *Journal of the History of Ideas*, XLIV (1983), 207-18.

18. Bénichou, Paul, 'La Démolition du héros', chapter IV in *Morales du Grand Siècle* (Paris, Gallimard, 1948).

19. ———, 'L'Intention des *Maximes*', in *L'Ecrivain et ses travaux* (Paris, José Corti, 1967), 3-37.

20. Coulet, Henri, 'La Rochefoucauld ou la peur d'être dupe', in *Hommage au doyen Etienne Gros* (Publications de la Faculté des Lettres d'Aix, Gap, Ophrys, 1959), 105-12.

21. Culler, Jonathan, 'Paradox and the Language of Morals in La Rochefoucauld', *Modern Language Review*, 68 (1973), 28-39.

22. Delft, Louis van, 'La Rochefoucauld, moraliste mondain', *Studi francesi*, XXIV (1980), 415-25.

23. ———, 'Pour une lecture mondaine de La Rochefoucauld. La caractérologie d'un moraliste pair de France', in *Images de La Rochefoucauld* (see *13* above), 145-57.

24. Deprun, Jean, 'La Réception des Maximes dans la France des Lumières', in *Images de La Rochefoucauld* (see *13* above), 39-46.

25. Hippeau, Louis, *Essai sur la morale de La Rochefoucauld* (Paris, Nizet, 1967).

26. James, E.D., 'Scepticism and Positive Values in La Rochefoucauld', *French Studies*, XXIII (1969), 349-61.

27. Kruse, Margot, 'Sagesse et folie dans l'œuvre des moralistes', *Cahiers de l'Association Internationale des Etudes Françaises*, XXX (1978), 121-37.
28. Lafond, Jean, *La Rochefoucauld: augustinisme et littérature*, 3e édition, 1986 (Paris, Klincksieck, 1977).
29. Moore, W.G., 'La Rochefoucauld: une nouvelle anthropologie', *Revue des Sciences Humaines*, 72 (1953), 301-10.
30. ———, *La Rochefoucauld: his mind and art* (Oxford, Clarendon Press, 1969).
31. Mourgues, Odette de, *Two French Moralists: La Rochefoucauld and La Bruyère* (Cambridge, Cambridge University Press, 1978).
32. Starobinski, Jean, 'La Rochefoucauld et les morales substitutives', *Nouvelle Revue Française* (1966), 16-34 and 211-29.
33. ———, 'Complexité de La Rochefoucauld', *Preuves* (mai 1962), 33-40.

THE MAXIM

34. Lafond, Jean, 'Mentalité et discours de maîtrise, ou le moraliste en question', *Romanistische Zeitschrift für Literaturgeschichte*, XII (1988), 314-26.
35. Lewis, Philip, *La Rochefoucauld: the art of abstraction* (Ithaca and London, Cornell University Press, 1977).
36. Mesnard, Jean, 'L'Esthétique de La Rochefoucauld', *Papers on French Seventeenth-Century Literature*, 37 (1987), 236-50.
37. Rosso, Corrado, *Procès à La Rochefoucauld et à la maxime* (Pisa, Editrice Libreria Goliardica; Paris, Nizet, 1986).
38. ———, *Saggezza in salotto: moralisti francesi ed espressione aforistica* (Naples, Edizioni Scientifiche Italiane, 1991).
39. Rousset, Jean, *La Littérature de l'âge baroque en France. Circé et le paon* (Paris, José Corti, 1954).

SEVENTEENTH- AND EIGHTEENTH-CENTURY WRITERS

40. Chamfort, *Maximes et pensées*, préface d'Albert Camus (Coll. Folio: Paris, Gallimard, 1982).
41. Esprit, Jacques, *La Fausseté des vertus humaines*, 2 vols (Paris, G. Desprez, 1677-78).
42. Fontenelle, *Nouveaux dialogues des morts*, ed. Jean Dagen (Paris, Didier, 1971).
43. Lafayette, Madame de, *La Princesse de Clèves*, ed. Peter Nurse (London, Harrap, 1970).
44. Pascal, *Pensées*, ed. Louis Lafuma (Paris, Editions du Seuil, 1962).
45. Segrais, *Mémoires anecdotes*, in *Œuvres diverses* (Amsterdam, 1723).

ADDENDUM

46. Clark, Henry C., *La Rochefoucauld and the language of unmasking* (Geneva, Droz, 1994).
47. Watts, Derek A., *La Rochefoucauld: Maximes* (Glasgow, University of Glasgow French and German Publications, 1993).

CRITICAL GUIDES TO FRENCH TEXTS

edited by
Roger Little, Wolfgang van Emden, David Williams